Wyoming's Cowboy Poets And Their Poetry

Introduction By
Gwen Petersen

Edited by
Jean Henry Mead

Medallion Books
Glenrock, Wyoming

© 2012 Medallion Books

All rights reserved.

First printing 2004

Second printing 2012

ISBN: 978-1-931415-33-0

The following poems have been previously published:

"After the Steers are Shipped," "Haying" and "Wintering," by Robert Roripaugh; *The Ranch*, University of Wyoming, Laramie, 2002.

"Lead Mare", "Blizzard," "Cattle, Horses, Sky and Grass" by Sue Wallis; *Green Grass Lover*, Dry Crik Press, Lemon Grove, CA, 1994.

"Rabbit Track Mind," "In a Mountain Shack Alone," by Georgie Sicking, *Just Thinking*, 1999.

"Cowboy Auction" by Jean Mathisen Haugen, won Lariet Laureatte award from Cowboypoetry.com, published in *Lander Journal*, 2003.

"Branding Day," "A Ride Across the Pasture," by Echo Roy, *Echoes in the Wind*, Sagebrush Echoes, Shoshoni, Wyoming.

"Please come to Wyoming," by John Nesbitt, *Black Hat Butte*, Leisure Books, 2003. "Nebraska Girl," by John Nesbitt, *For the Norden Boys*, Leisure Books, 2002.

"Abandoned Ranch," by Ron Bailey, *Horses I Have Known (and Wish I Hadn't)*, Aircraft Printers, Riverton, Wyoming 1991.

"Medicine Bow River," by Gene Shea, Poets Forum Magazine, 2003.

"A Heck of a Ride," by Rick Pitt, *Other Folks' Cowboy Poetry*, 2003; "Dallas" by Rick Pitt, *Other Folks' Cowboy Poetry*, 2003.

"The Bronc Ride" by Jo Fulton, *Fulton's Folly*, Hawk Book Company, Casper, Wyoming, 1991.

No part of this book may be reproduced or transmitted in any form or by any means, electronic or mechanical, including photocopying, recording, or any information or any storage or retrieval system, without written permission from the publisher.

Printed in the Western United States by Medallion Books

Dedication:

For all cowboy poets and those who love them and their poetry

Acknowledgements

My deepest appreciation to Gwen Petersen, who took time from her busy schedule to write the introduction for this book. My "many thanks" also to Jean Mathisen Haugen who brainstormed with me and pointed me in the right direction; to Echo Roy-Klaproth who added poets to my list; to Rhonda Sedgwick Stearns who added even more; to Andy Nelson who came through in a pinch and helped immeasurably; to Gene Shea who also made substitutions as well as everyone who allowed me to change a few words to make this book acceptable for young readers, for they are the future generation of cowboy poets.

Jean Henry Mead

Introduction

Cowboy and cowgal poets, from school age to those walking down their final trail, have contributed to and are continuing to add to language and folk literature in ways the rest of the world is gradually learning to appreciate.

In Wyoming's Cowboy Poets, cowboy bards present delicious servings of verse that will warm your heart, make you sigh, bring a tear to your eye and give you a reason to laugh out loud.

You can't always tell who's a cowboy poet or who is not. They don't have a "look." He or she probably doesn't wear an earring on the tongue or any other personal body part. They can, however, drive a stick shift, toss a lasso, and know what the south end of a cow looks like from the back of a horse.

See that lanky drink-of-water there in the worn jeans, the 5X Beaver broad-brimmed hat (or feed store cap) and boots or brogans? (Or maybe he's only tall when he's wearing his Stetson). Whether built high off the ground or closer to earth, a working cowboy can be identified by the sunburn on his face, the squint from watching horizons, his air of reserve and especially his light-up-the-world smile when he offers a grin and a howdy. He might also be a cowboy poet.

See that slim gal in the jeans and boots, tall hat or a feed store cap with a hole in the back to accommodate her pony tail? She might be wearing a platter size buckle on her belt, the award she received for winning the barrel-racing contest. Or maybe she's carrying the weight of added years, but she can still manage the ranch, the cowboys, the corrals and give you a quip a minute while doing so. She's the one who's always there to help out with the calving and lambing, the one who goes to town for parts, the one who handles the kitchen, the kids, and can ride for cattle with the best. A cowgirl does it all and can dance all night, too. She, too, might be a cowboy poet.

Those who write "cowboy poetry" are engaging in that mysterious creative act of putting on paper their thoughts, feelings and stories in rhyme and meter–though there are some superb versifiers out there who write non-rhyming "free verse" poems.

Some of my favorite rhyming poets (the dead ones) are Robert Service who produced volume after volume of verse telling the stories of his vagabond life from Europe to America to Mexico to the Yukon. Rudyard Kipling, whose works we all studied in school, created poetry that can make you weep or shiver or smile with delight. In Australia, Banjo Patterson wrote poems so powerful, movies have been made of them, "The Man From Snowy River" being the prime example.

Among my favorite live poets, you'll find many in Wyoming's Cowboy Poets. Jean Henry Mead has brought together a rich mixture of twenty-eight men and women cowboy poets, their biographies and their poetry. The result is an outstanding volume that you'll relish for years. What emerges, what radiates off the pages, what comes shining through—as the late Tom Eaton, a Montana cowboy poet said— "is the spirit of the poet."

Years ago at one of the early cowboy poetry gatherings, a man from a big city with tears in his eyes said, "I didn't know this was wonderful. I didn't know." The poetry had grabbed him by the heartstrings.

As the men and women in Wyoming's Cowboy Poets tell you their stories, their words let you understand their love of land, their pride in raising animals and tending crops, their timeless connection to seasons and weather and heartbreak and joy. It's all here. Just open and read. You won't be sorry.

Gwen Petersen

Contents

Robert Roripaugh	1
Sue Wallis	9
Chuck Larsen	17
Georgie Sicking	23
Charlie Firnekas	29
Rhonda Sedgwick Stearns	37
Mick Kaser	45
Jean Mathisen Haugen	53
Kent Stockton	61
Echo Roy-Klaproth	69
John Nesbitt	75
Ada McDonnel	81
Ron Bailey	87
Gene Shea	95
Leslie Keltner	101
Verlin Pitt	109
Rick Pitt	115
Terry Henderson	121
Garland C. Kennington	127
Lynne Hendrickson	133
Pete Davis	141
Honey DeFord	149
Stephen Langer	155
Robin Schupann	161
John Shreve	167
Josephine "Jo" Fulton	175
Andy Nelson	181
R.G. Sowers III	187
Gwen Peterson	193
Jean Henry Mead	195
Photo Credits	197

Robert Roripaugh

Robert Roripaugh

Wyoming's former poet laureate feels that readers and listeners in a cowboy poetry audience are enthusiastic about the "portrayal of western life and values in a time when Americans are becoming increasingly rootless and uncertain about the direction of their lives, occupations, and relationships to the land and the places where they live.

"Many of the people involved with cowboy poetry have past or present ties to western culture or ranch life themselves or through family, friendships, the places where they live, or the kind of work they do. There is also an appeal in poetry which can be understood the first time it is read or heard and the humor cowboy poetry often contains, as well as the vernacular and style in which it is written and performed."

Poetry is a Roripaugh family tradition. Robert was first introduced to the genre by his mother who loved and wrote poetry. She read volumes to her small son and bought him chapbooks as he grew older. His daughter, Lee Ann Roripaugh, is an accomplished poet "who began writing as a child, studied with good teachers at the University of Indiana, and won a National Poetry Series Prize in 1999 for a Wyoming volume titled *Beyond Heart Mountain*. In addition to her poetry, she teaches writing at the University of South Dakota. Her second poetry collection is titled *The Year of the Snake*.

Western poetry also came naturally to the Roripaughs. The second son of a mining engineer and school teacher, Robert Roripaugh was born in southern California during the Great Depression. When he was seven, his father moved his family to Midland, Texas, where they lived until World War II. They then relocated to Lander, Wyoming, to ranch.

Robert's father helped him develop an interest in firearms, hunting, fishing, archery, fly-tying and camping. He also inherited his father's interest in western history. "My mother taught me to value education and make use of my mind and imagination," he said, "and my father showed me the practical skills and knowledge from life itself that would strengthen my writing."

During high school, he played football "as an undersized left guard," and wrote for the school page in *The Sunday Reporter-Telegram*. Robert later attended the University of Texas as a journalism and geology major before transferring to the University of Wyoming, where he completed his B.A. degree in geology and M.A. in English.

During the summers, he worked at his family ranch, which he credits with his development as a writer. After army service, which included a year in Japan, he held a Coe Fellowship in American Studies at Wyoming and traveled twice to the land of the rising sun, where he married his wife, Yoshiko.

He then taught two years in New Mexico on a teaching assistantship in English. There he wrote short stories and began work on a novel about the occupation of Japan, which was published as *A Fever for Living* by William Morrow in 1961, and reprinted by Dell on this side of the Atlantic as well as in England.

His second novel, *Honor Thy Father*, an historic look at cattle ranching in Wyoming's Sweetwater River area, received the Western Heritage Award from the National Cowboy Hall of Fame as the outstanding western novel for 1963. The author also published Wyoming short stories in literary magazines such as *The Atlantic Monthly, Sage, South Dakota Review, Quarterly West,* and *Writers Forum*. During the fall of 1958, he was hired by the University of Wyoming, where he spent the next thirty-eight years teaching writing and literature. He said, "I was happy to be back in the state and closer to our ranch, which my father and mother would still own for another six years."

Along the way he held a number of short term jobs such as carpentry, horse wrangling for a pack-trip outfit, ranch, and oilfield work. His first cowboy poem was written while a student in a University of Wyoming writing class, and published in a campus literary magazine.

"Before cowboy poetry became widely recognized in the 1980s as a distinct and popular kind of folk poetry celebrating western life and culture, I was writing poems about ranch life in Wyoming as I had known it on my parent's place and other ranches in the Lander Valley, as well as in the colorful western town where we came to shop, buy supplies, and pick up our mail."

His poetry has appeared in two volumes: *Learn to Love the Haze* and *The Ranch*, which placed first in the Wyoming State Historical Society for fine Arts of 2003, and was a finalist in the Western Writers of America Spur awards of 2002. His essays and articles have also been published in literary magazines and the Wyoming Cultural Guide for 2001, sponsored by the Council on the Arts; and others.

"The most creative piece of nonfiction I've written," he said, was 'Wyoming Ranch Life Thirty Years Ago,' which was included in Judith Sandoval's Historic Ranches of Wyoming."

Most of his poems have been set in Wyoming and deal with people, ways of life, and experiences he's had or learned about here. "Ranching and small-town life in the area where I lived with my parents along the Wind River Mountains have always been an influence on my writing."

Robert Roripaugh was named Wyoming's Poet Laureate in 1995 by Governor Jim Geringer. He served the state in that capacity until 2002. "Along with continuing to write about Wyoming and giving readings or workshops," he said, "I wanted to do programs which would give audiences a greater appreciation and knowledge of the poets and their poetry that strengthened the state's literary history."

The poet's contributions to this collection include "After the Steers are Shipped," "Haying," and "Wintering," which were selected from his award winning book, *The Ranch*.

After the Steers are Shipped

After the steers have been shipped,
Deer slip into our lower meadow—
Soft dun against willows, pale grass.

Starlings arranged ceremoniously in
Cottonwoods patch sky beyond the creek.
By the road to town, chokecherries

Are deeper green, limbs sagging with
Purple fruit. Before the first
Easy frost, an old black car appears.

Mr. Wallowingbull, his daughters,
Borrow the stepladder to climb among
Dark-leaved branches. That green

Mixes with blue jeans, a red bandana,
Long skirts, as chokecherries stain
Hands, rungs of the ladder . . . ground.

When we go down to repair the water-
Trap fence, birds fly up noisily
And deer become earth, grass, sky.

Haying

Grass meets the sickle-bar,
Falls, a swatch circling meadow,

Forming tighter swatches
Of brome and timothy

As clattering tractors level
The morning's dimension,

Uncut fields roll across
My eyes like summer,

Frightened pheasants hurdle
Out of weedy ditches,

And sun heats the sky
To blue steel above green

Falling into feed for rakes,
Cattle nosing through the snow.

Wintering

I.
A foot of snow falls.
In the silent meadow cattle gather,
Waiting for the red hay wagon.

II.
Riding alone on New Year's,
My father finds fifty deer huddled
Below the warm brown cliffs.

III.
Our horses wander off into
A storm. For days Bud feeds them:
"They aren't hurting nothing."

IV.
Drifts cover the wild roses.
By morning pheasants roost on snow,
A prism for winter sunlight.

Sue Wallis

Sue Wallis

Reared on a ranch at Recluse, Wyoming, Sue Wallis McQueary still ranches although "like many agricultural people of today, we call ourselves ranchers but the truth is that we have to seek outside work to keep our families healthy. For us, that means I run equipment in an open pit coal mine, and my husband hauls oil in the oil patch."

Before moving back to her family ranch in 1999, Sue made her living as a non-profit arts administrator at the Western Folklore Center in Elko, Nevada, where she managed the well-known Cowboy Poetry Gathering. As a divorced mother of three, she attended the University of Wyoming American Studies Program prior to her thirtieth birthday.

Sue Wallis grew up surrounded by "readers, writers and thinkers. My dad loved poetry, especially Kipling, and I recall a winter, when I was probably eight or nine, when Dad decided to memorize the "Ballad of East and West." To do this, he would teach himself a new stanza by repeating it over and over aloud at the breakfast table. He would then practice while driving our team of Belgians and the hay sled from one hay corral to the next. That winter we were feeding a thousand heifers on the Bitter Creek side of the ranch, and it would take two full days to get them all fed.

"We would feed up the creek one day and down the creek the next, so it took all day. The hay corrals and each bunch of heifers were a mile or so apart so there was lots of practice time in-between for the lengthy poem. Until the day I die, I will remember him with his wide-legged stance, the lines to Ulysses S. Grant and Robert E. Lee loose and swaying— they knew the routine as well as the rest of us. Us kids were sitting along the back of the sled with the snow swishing past under our feet, jingle of harness, warm, sweet aroma of horse sweat and hay in crisp air, and him bellowing out:

"Oh, East is East, and West is West,
tho never the twain shall meet,
Till Earth and Sky stand presently at God's
great judgment seat,
But there is neither East nor West,
nor border, nor breed, nor birth
When two strong men stand face to face,
though they come from the ends of the Earth."

Before the age of twelve, Sue began writing limericks as well as a poem titled, "An Ode to a Rose," which ran six handwritten pages. "Rose was a pretty good rhyming word," she said. "Unfortunately, none of this amazing early literary effort survives."

Her own favorite poets include Paul Zarzyski "for his passion, wide open exuberance, and high kicking, bronco riding style; the late Buck Ramsey for beautifully, precise technical excellence, and sly use of Pushkin's schemes in West Texas cowboy epics." Next she lists her husband, Rod McQueary, "for his courage in writing and healing the wounds of Vietnam, and because he makes me laugh every day." Baxter Black also makes her laugh and Waddie Mitchell makes her think. Elizabeth Ebert is another favorite "because she just gets it so right."

Creativity is a family tradition. Her husband, she said, "is one of the finest poets and writers, in my opinion, this country has ever seen—he nourishes my soul every day, encourages me, supports me, and edits for me." Her mother, Myrt Wallis, "is also a fine writer, artist and poet" and two of her children, Isaac and Ceci, have literary talent. Her grandmother wrote family memoirs and another ancestor, who settled with her husband on the Laramie plains, published a chapbook of poetry.

The poet writes because "she loves the sound of the language, the lay of words and syllables and images. The cadence of human communication, and the ability to evoke a time, a place, and emotion just fascinates me. I write whenever I feel like it, which is about every day that I'm not at work, or busy at the ranch. I have no schedule whosoever. For me, writing and thinking about writing, is a big part of my spiritual practice."

She concluded that nearly everyone she encounters, and virtually anything she experiences, can inspire her to write. "Besides the cow country poets and writers that surround us today, I am mightily inspired by the classics–Dickinson, Whitman, Keats, Sylvia Plath and Pablo Neuda, Rumi, Robert Louis Stevenson, and Robert Service, Badger Clark and S. Omar Barker." Maya Angelou, Ernest Hemingway, Jack Kerouac, and Jimmy Buffett are also on her list, as well as many others.

Her poems, "Lead Mare, "Blizzard," and "Cattle, Horses, Sky and Grass" are featured here.

Lead Mare

That woman there
She could be a lead mare
Has watched horses so long
And so well she can tell what goes on
In their minds

It's that high-thrown head
How she holds her shoulders
Watch . . . she'll kinda hunch them
Throw her weight in ways
Unseen by us, but understood
By the saddle bunch

Once she tried it in Kentucky
That lead mare bit
And it worked there, too
At one of those fancy outfits
White board fences
Blooded thoroughbreds
She slipped away from the crowd
Stood quiet, moved her body
And they all quit grazing
Tossed her head
And they all came to her
Just like they do

At the ranch

Blizzard

Yup . . .
It's one of those bono fide
Wet and sloppy freezing plaster
Blowing horizontal
Storms

You gotta kinda conjure up survival
One reflector pole
At a time

(And trust your luck)

Thank all the gods
That you don't have to be a-horseback
or open buggy bound for home
Tonight

Think how two stiff drinks
and one hot bath
Will help your fearful clinching eyes

Blizzard-beaten mind
And your sore and aching muscles
Soften and relax

Then . . . you can laugh
At Old Man Winter's dying blast
Howling futilely outside
With deadly
Malice

(And just be glad that you're alive)

Cattle, Horses, Sky and Grass

Cattle, horses, sky and grass—
these are the things that sway and pass
before our eyes and through our dreams,
through shiny, sparkly, golden gleams
within our psyche that find and know
the value of this special glow
that only gleams for those who bleed
their sole and heart and utter need
into the mightily, throbbing Earth
from which springs life and death and birth.
These cattle, horses, grass and sky
dance and dance and never die—
they circle through the realms of air
and ground and empty spaces where
a human being can join the song—
can circle, too, and not go wrong
amidst the natural, pulsing forces
of sky and grass and cows and horses.

This chant of Life cannot be heard,
it must be felt, there is no word
to sing that could express the true
significance of how we wind
through all these hoops of Earth and mind—
through horses, cattle, sky and grass
and all these things that sway and pass.

Chuck Larsen

Chuck Larsen

"Most folks grew up being in love with the West," Chuck Larsen said, and "although I grew up on a farm, I always leaned toward the cattle and horse side of the business. The genre of cowboy poetry simply continues to pump life into that same romance."

The Saratoga, Wyoming, general manager of a rural electric cooperative grew up in eastern South Dakota, the eldest of three children. His paternal grandfather was "a master at telling a story" and passed the talent on to his son, a playwright, "so I came by it naturally," he said.

"As a boy, we made a trip to town every Saturday, with eggs, cream and a grocery list. That trip also included stops at the small public library where my dad encouraged all of us at an early age to get our own library card and to read. It was one of his greatest contributions to me that, through those books, he helped me to travel to so many places and to grow an imagination." He didn't write his first cowboy poem until a friend in Cody, Wyoming, convinced him to attend a cowboy poetry and range ballads program at the museum.

"Sitting in the audience after listening to several cowboy poets, I got to thinking, "I can do this. So I went back home and wrote a few poems." He returned to Cody the following year, "recited a couple, got some applause, and the rest is history. I was hooked." His poetry has since been published in *American Cowboy Magazine* and he has performed at gatherings and symposiums at Encampment, Riverton, Rawlins, Devils Tower and Cheyenne, Wyoming; Valentine, Nebraska; Durango and Arvada, Colorado; Elko, Nevada; and Ogden, Utah.

Larsen's favorite poet is R. P. Smith, a Broken Bow, Nebraska, resident, "who tells it like it is. I really like the way he writes. It's honest, filled with family values and it's to the point. He can make me laugh and make me swallow hard. It's that emotion thing. There are so many other poets that I truly respect and appreciate, so picking just one is really difficult."

Composing poetry "mainly boils down to 'emotion" and that can be either something that strikes me funny or something that tugs at a few of my heart strings. Time is also a big factor. The winter months are the most productive for me. Summers are filled up with day to day work, then trying to fit in breaking colts, pack trips, announcing a few rodeos, and traveling around performing."

When asked what he treasures most, other than family and pets, he listed his scrapbooks, family photos and albums. "So much of what they contain link me to my past and what I am. Everything else can be replaced."

His poem, "Treasures by the Hat-Full" follows.

Treasures by the Hat-Full

We spend our evenin's in the bunkhouse,
Fillin' that gap between day and night.
Talkin', sharin' the events of our lives.
Until somebody'd douse the light.

Sooner or later it always happens,
Somebody'd bring up the old man again.
We'd talk about all he'd done,
About all the things he'd been.

Like how old was he really?
I guess nobody ever cared.
We'd all joshed about his age,
But to ask, nobody ever dared.

He'd been a hand here forever,
And when somethin' ancient met his view,
The old man would reminisce, rememberin'
He'd been there when it was new.

He'd proudly wore a sweat stained hat,
Branded Stetson, styled Open-Road.
Levis faded, turned up at the cuff,
Boots of a ride, heeled, pointed toed.

We'd sit and talk of the old man,
In laughter and in reverent tones.
Of horses he'd ridden and outlived,
Now scattered memories and bones.

We remembered how he'd said goodbye,
His final moment held at bay.
One by one he'd called us in,
Near death he'd had his say.

To Tom he'd passed his spurs,
To Ed his worn silver bit.
To Frank he gave his weathered saddle,
His boots to whoever they would fit.

Just a kid, scared as heck,
I'd stood there alone by his bed.
Hat in hand, heart throat high,
And listened to the words he said.

"What I'm givin' up are just things.
The real treasurers are in my mind.
I'll be takin' those with me now,
Takin' them, yet leavin' them behind.

"I'm talkin' about everyday treasures,
Those I've stolen, but never really took.
They're right smack in front of you,
If you'll take the time to look.

"Like all those stars shinin' at night,
Or the rosy glow of a dawnin' sky.
Whispered colors of aspens in the fall,
Just take them, never askin' why.

"Like the walk of an honest horse,
On a day when the weather's good.
Like livin' the life I've lived,
Satisfied in knowin' that I could.

"Heck, kid, I'm just an old man,
Neither profound, all knowin' or wise.
See, I've just lived my whole life,
With open ears and open eyes.

"It's these secrets I'm leavin' you,
Along with this old hat of mine.
Look over my string of horses too,
Baldy and Nate might suit you fine."

I took the old man's cherished hat,
Along with his offered up advice.
I started gathering my treasures,
Things that come without a price.

Today I brushed an old bald-faced horse,
Over near the horse corral water gap.
Hearin' the water dance, tumble and fall,
On it's way along life's treasure map.

Tonight if we talk of the old man,
I won't be telling them of our chat.
Like life's treasures, it's somethin'
I'm still keepin' under "his" old hat.

Georgi Sicking

Georgie Sicking

Gerogie Connell Sicking has been called "a mare among the geldings," but she preferred to be called a cowboy because she worked alongside other ranch hands, performing the same tasks and experiencing similar hardships with her male counterparts.

"Cowgirls are the ones who wear the clothes and smile," she said. "Cowboys are the ones who do the work and to be a cowboy is to take in all kinds of occupations. You need to be a little bit of a lawyer, pretty much a doctor, a teacher, and a psychologist.

"There's always the chance when you get bucked off of getting a broken neck, back or leg. You can get tangled in a rope, kicked by a horse, and hooked by a cow. My dad was dragged to death by a horse. Being a cowboy is dangerous business."

Georgie was bucked off a number of times, most recently when she broke her clavicle. She also lost four men in her family to accidents, including her husband and youngest son. Despite the danger, she continued to ride her two horses although legally blind.

Born and reared on a ranch in Arizona, Georgie broke her first wild mustang when she was nine, and remembers telling her older sister at the age of five that "when I grow up I want to be a good hand in a cowboy outfit in spite of being a girl. Someday I want a ranch of my own.' My sister said, 'Those are boys' ideas and you can't have 'em.' And I said, 'Boys' ideas or not, I've got 'em.'"

She fulfilled her dream of being a top hand and owning her own ranch, but the process wasn't easy. Most ranchers would not allow her to work with the men and the women who knew her tried to discourage her by saying that no man wanted to marry a tom boy, that she should dress and act like a young lady.

Her family moved to Kingman, Arizona, so that she and her siblings could attend high school, but Georgie quit after her second year because she wasn't learning what she craved: cowboying. Her principal, who didn't try to talk her out of leaving, offered her this advice: "Keep your rope off other people's cattle."

The pretty girl roped herself a husband at 17, but the marriage only lasted four months because, although the young couple gathered wild burros and sold them for $2.50 a head, "he couldn't catch one. That's the way to get rid of a husband, out rope him," she said. Two years later she married a handsome cowboy, Frank Sicking, whom she worked alongside for the next thirty-four years in Arizona and Nevada. She then ranched alone.

Georgie began writing cowboy poetry at the age of 17, whenever she was in cow camp. "I'm not prolific," she said. "I've only written sixty or seventy poems," but she has been invited to perform in countless poetry gatherings all over the West, and was awarded the Gail Gardner Award for outstanding working cowboy poet while in her sixties.

She was also inducted into the Cowgirl Hall of Fame

in 1989 in Hereford, Texas; and the mayor of Rawlins, Wyoming, presented her with a gold key to the city.

During the summer of 2003, Georgie performed in Texas, New Mexico, Arizona, Nevada, Oregon and Washington; traveling alone or with a friend, Rhonda Sedgwick Stearns. People are surprised that someone her age with macular degeneration would travel alone but the "cowboy" is determined not to let her handicap stop her from traveling.

The government forced her into selling her ranch when she was 75, because the Kiwi bird habitat was endangered. She paid off her debts and shipped her remaining cattle to a small ranch she purchased in northern California, where she remained until January of 2000, when she lost her driver's license and decided that she needed to be near her daughter in Kaycee, Wyoming.

She wasn't there long before the Middle Fork of the Powder River flooded and destroyed her home, located on two and a half acres along the bank. Undeterred, Georgie moved in a mobile home, and continued to ride her horses which were stabled on the property.

An hour-long documentary film has since been produced about her life as well as a book titled "A Mare Among the Geldings." A book of her poetry is also on book store shelves and Georgie Connell Sicking continued to enjoy her life "one day at a time."

Her contributions to this collection include "Rabbit Track Mind" and "In a Mountain Shack Alone."

Rabbit Track Mind

I got myself a cow dog, one of the working kind
He had all the looks and he had all the moves,
 but he had a rabbit track mind.

Now most of the time he would mind
pretty good and stay at my horse's heels
Till a rabbit jumped up and away
he'd go, trying to catch him a meal.

Right through the middle of the cattle,
yapping all the way
Scattering them from here to yonder
And all I could do was pray

That he would hear my pleas of desperation
And come on back and help me
out of a scattered situation.

He finally lost the rabbit and came on
back, his owner for to find
Helped me gather the cattle up,
but still had a rabbit track mind.

Now I have known a few people
like that, and success I may never find
Because of one simple affliction
and that is a rabbit track mind.

In a Mountain Shack Alone

You're all alone in a mountain shack
Many miles from town,
'Tis the fall of the year
And you can hear the leaves fall softly down.

A cricket chirps, and an old cow bawls
To a calf that's somewhere near,
As you sit alone on a moonlit night
These and other night sounds you hear.

Then you sort of get to thinking
As you sit there all alone,
And wonder how those others are
That once formed a well-loved home;

You think of things you have known
Or someone who to you is dear,
And you wonder how it would be
If they were only near.

You sometimes think of something
you've said or done
To hurt some well liked friend
That caused a quarrel or a deep, deep hurt
And brought a valued friendship to an end.

'Tis there you'll find another side
of a person you thought you had known,
But you'll find you know yourself much better
After a month in a mountain shack alone.

Charlie Firnekas

Charlie Firnekas

The grandson of early Wyoming freighters, Charlie was born in Bufallo, the fourth of six offspring of Church and Maggy Firnekas, who ranched on the edge of the Hole in the Wall canyon. His maternal great-grandfather was an early freighter who "helped to clean up the mess" following the Battle of the Little Big Horn. He also served as sheriff and held other government jobs in Converse County.

Charlie's maternal grandfather operated the stage between Kaycee and Arminto, "pretty raw country in the winter. He sometimes took a pack horse to deliver first class mail to Kaycee. The route was a three-day round trip when he drove the stage." Charlie's father was "an old time cowboy and real pioneer" who repeated stories told to him by his own father about participants in the Johnson County War as well as ranchers and outlaws who lived and traveled through the Hole in the Wall canyon.

His mother lived with her family near Guernsey and

Charlie recalls her telling of their move to the Kaycee area on foot. "They would roll their beds out at night [on the sagebrush-covered prairie]," he said. "They were pretty rugged people."

Following in his ancestors' bootprints, Charlie still ranches his parent's cattle spread. He turned down a sports scholarship in high school to further his education, choosing instead to work the ranch where he spent most of his life.

The rancher laughed when he compared modern cowboys with old-timers. "If we're going to be realistic, we ought to put the four-wheeler and microwave oven in the cowboy hall of fame," he said. "I spent a lot of time in camp when the only way you got there was on horseback unless you went on foot. You had no choice and you knew the next day was gonna be the same. You changed horses in the middle of the day because you rode 'em down. It's not an easy life, but it's a good life."

The cowboy's poems include stories passed down by his ancestors. Charlie decided to try writing cowboy poetry following an invitation to attend a gathering and cowboy music festival in Newcastle, Wyoming. "I sat down and wrote a few lines of poetry that rhymed, then took my guitar and went over there," he said. He has since performed at cowboy poetry gatherings in Newcastle, Kaycee, Sheridan and Riverton, Wyoming. He has also performed as a solo act or "with others" in Buffalo, Kaycee, Gillette and Esterbrook.

Charlie plays several musical instruments and performs with three other musicians at various locations within the state, often performing his own songs. "I write because of things around me," he said. "I'm not the least bit interested in the Hollywood type of cowboy or off color stuff that seems to be part of it."

Badger Clark's work has been his favorite "because he

seemed to make things come alive." But his main concern and focus outside of ranching is performing "old time music" and writing anything that catches his fancy.

His poems "Hole in the Wall" and "Champion" were selected for inclusion in this volume for their historic significance. Nate Champion, a suspected rustler, was shot to death by fifty cattlemen and Texas mercenaries after they killed his companions and set fire to his cabin during the Johnson County War of 1892. Charlie Firnekas claims that Hole in the Wall rancher Bob Smith was shot in the back by lawman Joe LeFors, when CY cowboys accompanied him and ranch foreman Bob Devine into the Hole to retrieve stolen cattle five years later. There are many versions of what actually happened in both incidents, but one thing is certain. Resentment is still apparent among those whose roots run generations deep in the area.

Hole in the Wall

There's a place on the east of the Big Horns
that they call the Hole in the Wall,
And just how the name came to be
really don't matter at all.

A trail goes over the red wall
Where once the outlaws did ride
There's lots of places around there
That furnish a good place to hide.

There's many a myth and story
And many a down right lie
About the men that made it famous
How they lived and how they did die.

You've all heard about Butch and Sundance,
How the Wild Bunch plundered and stole
But there's way more told about them
Than what we know was their role.

There's a place in Powder River Canyon
That's called the outlaw cave.
It wasn't just named that by chance
There was plenty of outlaws to save.

Bob Smith in those days gone by
Met his death at the hands of a gun.
He died there at the Hole in the Wall,
That's where that it was done.

There's a new bunch of desperados
That call themselves the Hole in the Wall gang,
They're a hard bitten bunch of fellers
Like what most of the songs have sang.

They put on their bug repellant
And drink all that high-priced booze
Then hook on to their horse trailers
And pull on their boots—
this ain't no place for shoes.

These guys are still making history
Though they act different this time around.
They have a portable bar along
And we know when they're in town.

Champion

They don't seem to name nothin' for him,
Like the men that shot him down.
They claim that he was a "rustler,"
And they didn't want him around.

They tried to kill him at night
At a cave at the mouth of the canyon,
He woke with his gun a blazin'
And put them killers on the run.

Well, they got an army together,
A good lot of them "hired guns."
Nate and Nick were at the KC Ranch
Along with two other ones.

They caught the men with Nate and Nick
When they went out early next day,
When Nick went out to look for them
They shot him and left him lay.

Nate drug him back in the cabin
and that is where he died.
Fifty odd men were shooting at him
While Nate held them off from inside.

Well, he held them off all day
'Til along just before night fall,
He kept a diary telling about it
It didn't sound like no fun at all.

He wrote the name of the man he knew
He said it was lonesome in there
That he'd try to make a run for it
When it got dark he might have a prayer.

They pushed a wagon they set ablaze
Down to light the cabin on fire,
To end Nate Champion's life
Was the "invader's" number one desire.

Nate wrote they had fired the cabin
And he knew that the time had come,
When he'd have to make a run for it
So he wrote a farewell to his chums.

They found him a ways from the ruins
His body was riddled with lead
With a note that said, "Rustlers beware,"
Now at last this brave man was dead.

They took the bodies to Buffalo
To the north, forty odd miles away
Four hundred eighty-three people paid homage,
When they laid Nate and Nick in their graves.

I don't know how Nate lived.
I only know how he died.
Let's turn that coin over.
It should say "Champion" on one side.

Rhonda Sedgwick-Stearns

Rhonda Sedgwick Stearns

Inducted into the National Cowgirl Hall of Fame in 1977 at Hereford, Texas, Rhonda Sedgwick was, at that time, the youngest honoree and the first from her home state of Wyoming. Honored for her all-around cowgirl qualities, including every aspect of ranch work, she was recognized for her horsemanship as well as the breeding, breaking and training of horses.

Rhonda has always been on horseback. Reared as an only child, she was carried on a pillow on her mother's saddle from the time she was two weeks old, and rode her own horse up to twenty miles a day when she was two.

The majority of her education came from "horses and cows, rough country, good hands, and true Christian folk who live their sermons instead of preaching them," she said. Her schooling was earned from Calvert correspondence courses and three years "in a schoolhouse. I never went to college. The only reason I wanted to go was to rodeo and I figured that was a poor excuse to spend that much money.

I could rodeo without being in college."

The cowgirl taught horsemanship, successfully competed in horse show performance classes with both Quarter horses and Appaloosas, and judged and announced horse shows. A rodeo contestant in several events, she performed during high school at both the amateur and professional levels, earning national titles. She was also a state and national rodeo queen and found time to serve as a rodeo organist. Rhonda was the first woman for many years to hold an RCA card to play the organ at top pro rodeos across the nation.

As a journalist, she published articles about cowboys, horses, rodeos and other western events. Her cowboy poetry began during her late teens when she wrote "Night Before Christmas on the Ranch" for the National High School Rodeo Association newspaper.

Her second poem, "Cowboy's Lament," was written for a dying wrangler. The poetic account of the cowhand's stories was so well liked that he "made his poor wife read it to him several times a day."

The cowgirl admits that "the desperate need for money motivates me to write everything but poetry." Poetry is "pure emotion" with a "deep love of the cowboying lifestyle and all that pertains to it . . . the land, people, animals, skills, history and experiences."

The poet does ranch day work with her husband Will, whom she considers a "great storyteller." When she's not teaching horsemanship clinics, announcing rodeos and horse shows, she plays piano and organ and conducts "a little preaching" in various churches in eastern Wyoming. She also hosts a radio show. In her spare time, she operates her own publishing business, Quarter Circle A Enterprises—the name taken from her brand—and edits manuscripts when the occasion arises. Her husband's 88-year-old father and 92-year-mother lived in her home, and she cared for them as well.

Rhonda has performed at cowboy poetry gatherings in South Dakota, Idaho, New Mexico, Texas, and her home state of Wyoming, and has somehow found time to write thousands of articles for rodeo magazines, ranch and horse journals. She pens a weekly column of horse news for *Tri-State Livestock News* as well as feature articles. She also published, *Sky Trails: The Life of Clyde W. Ice; Prairie Trails of Miz Mac, Trails of a Wanderer: The Keith W. Avery Story,* and *Mush Creek Musings,* a chapbook of her poems. She is currently working on a book about bull riders, the first in a series. Her cowboy poetry includes: "The Jing Jangs" and "Life's Answers."

THE JING-JANGS

He said he'd been out in the jing-jangs
An' the kid sort'a looked at him strange—
This stove-up, wind-dried ol' relic
Of the wild, wide Wyoming range.

"Now, where in the heck is the jing-jangs?
The kid snickered, aside, to his friends.
"I reckon, son," said the old one,
"It's someplace you ain't never been.

"Most likely y' never will see it,
'Cause it's range y'r trails won't never cross—
An' surely that's best in the long run,
'Cause out there you'd dang sure be lost!

"It lays a bit North of 'blue yonder,'
An' West of the place rainbows end—
A country that most folk don't know of,
Where wide, rolling vistas begin.

"It's home to the elk an' the bobcat,
Where mule deer an' whitetail abound,
An' thanks to the dear God who made it
There ain't many people around.

"Just those that He chose to be stewards—
The few that He knows understands
How precious an' rare is the priv'lege
To dwell deep in the heart of this land.

"Folk tuned to the rhythms of nature
An' toughened by all her extremes—
Perched on the raw edge of 'existin',
A people who never would dream

"Of whinin' demandin' or strikin'
If things wasn't goin' their way—
Or even think of complainin'
Of the work they must do ev'ry day.

"'Cause they was all raised up on 'rugged',
An' 'easy' is a term they don't ken—
The kind of soft livin' you fellers has known
To them would be vergin' on sin.

"As for me, son, I thrive on ranch work—
So I think like the horse an' the cow—
To my mind they are lots smarter
Than mankind that dwells in big towns.

"But, I've not told y'much of the jing jangs . . .
'Cause it ain't somethin' y'spit out in words—
It's more in my heart an' gut than may be . . .
In a pony's eye . . . an' the jingle of spurs.

"It's felt in y'r throat as y' watch five bull elk
Spooked from bed in the misty blue dawn . . .
Or sit still on y'r horse to watch a parade
Of ten curious antelope fawns.

"A' passin' so close you could spit in their eye,
As they sniff y'r strange scent on the air . . .
It's the coil an' the buzz of the rattler . . .
It's a feelin', I guess . . . an' it's rare!

"But if I was a prince or a ruler—
Or a rich man with never a care—
Who could pick any place on this planet,
I vow, son, I'd rather be there . . .

"An' that's where I'm headin' right now, boy,
'Cause my belly's plumb full 'a this town—
An' I'll stay out there, in the jing-jangs . . .
If only the Lord will allow."

Life's Answers

Two cowboys, old and weathered
With the skin of leather hue,
Sat lazily in rockin' chairs
Admiring' the sunset view.

The one said, "Pard, I wonder
What good our lives have been.
Was there some purpose, plot or plan . . .
Or banner for us to win?"

The other spat and grunted,
"We've rode the trail plumb straight.
We've done each job the best we could,
An' we shore don't dread our fate."

"I reckon that's contentment–
What money cannot buy–
An' life can't hold no finer prize,
For anyone's grit an' try."

A chuckle came in answer,
"Yew always did think deep;
Them are the thoughts that's in my head
Each night as I fall asleep."

I cain't spit 'em out that way
All smooth an' purrin' like;
But it's pure truth–an' all that counts–
In this sunset time of life."

Mick Kaser

Mick Kaser

Ranchester, Wyoming, rancher Mike Kaser spent his formative years on the Hidden River Ranch north of Egbert, thirty miles east of Cheyenne, where Lodgepole Creek, "the longest in the United States," wound its way through the ranch's center. The creek sinks beneath the surface during the fall, forming a subsurface aquifer 50 feet deep and 150 feet wide, "hence the name: Hidden River Ranch."

Mick was the eldest of four sons who helped his parents raise purebred Herefords, and had a small herd of his own. He attended Cheyenne Community College, the University of Wyoming, Oregon Technical Institute, and Montana State University at Bozeman, "but only graduated from Burns High School, 23 miles east of Cheyenne." He subsequently worked as a surveyor, "a lands man," and coordinated statewide programs. He also guided hunters in the Big Horn Mountains, worked in civil engineering, "ranched and farmed a little." When interviewed, he was building a house south of Ranchester, mainly with his own labor.

His wife was teaching school across the state border on the Indian Reservation at Wyola, Montana; and his son was a college student in Casper. The Kasers own a small ranch on Wyoming's Tongue River where they primarily raise hay, "with a few head of cattle now and then."

His poetry began when he wrote a Christmas poem in lieu of a letter, a practice that has continued. In 1993, an agent in Rawlins, Wyoming, helped to organize the first Gem City Jamboree Cowboy Poetry Gathering in Laramie, and Mick wrote two Wyoming historical poems for the event, circa 1800s. As a result, he has been featured twice at the Elko, Nevada, gathering as well events at Arvada, Nebraska; Rawlins and Sheridan, Wyoming, and a number of towns in between.

"I used to drive a lot of miles and that's when I was inspired," he said. "I carried a pocket recorder and with no distractions and miles of sagebrush, it's pretty easy to let your imagination go to work." Some of his inspiration comes from books and tapes of other poets, among them Robert Service. He said, "I read his book three times."

His all-time favorite is S. Omar Barker. Mick feels that Baxter Black is "probably the best humorist/entertainer" in the genre, but considers Waddie Mitchell a better poet and performer. Wally McRae and Leo Buffman are also high on his list.

The poet has produced a tape of his own as well as a book titled, *Horses to Cattle–And that Old Wilson Saddle*. He now pens his poetry "whenever I get some time and can find a little solitude."

Mick Kaser describes his humor as dry, and lists poetry and Wyoming history as his favorite hobbies. He combines the two in his poem, an account of the Battle of Tongue River. The battle took place at the end of August in 1865 when General Conner and his cavalrymen destroyed an Arapaho village, killing more than fifty tribesman and destroying their tents, clothing, and winter food supply. "Bugles on the Mornin'" is his poetic version of what happened that day on the campground now within sight of his barn.

Bugles on the Mornin'

As I look out of the back door
of the barn here at the place
My mind begins to wander
Back in time, events retraced

As I gaze across the meadow
Where we now put up some hay
I wonder just what happened here
one hot summer day

On a summer's eve in August
You might hear the cannon roarin'
And the rattlin' sound of sabers
And the Bugles on the mornin'

It was August eighteen sixty-five
Right near the Bozeman Trail
Where Wolf Creek meets Tongue River
In a long green grassy Trail

Black Bear and Old David
Chiefs of the Arapaho
Were breakin' camp that mornin'
In the fiery sunrise glow

When the volunteers from Iowa
Emerged from Tongue River
Jaded horses faltered
Weakened muscles quivered

As they charged across the meadow
Springfield rifles blazin'
Where three thousand Indian ponies
Stood, peacefully a grazin'

Terrified, the Indians scattered
Their peaceful village razed
The cavalry split their ranks
And all went different ways

There were soldiers chasing warriors
There were ponies on the run
Squaws and children taking refuge
Up Wolf Creek, up the Tongue

They hid the kids down in the willows
Then fled up Wolf Creek
Old Black Bear baited Conner
'cause he knew his mounts were weak

A forced march the night before
Now began to take its toll
Conner had just fourteen men
When he turned and took a poll

So, when Black Bear had him stretched out
Three miles, or maybe four
He turned and fell upon them
And gave new meaning to this war

Of a sudden, the attackers
Now became the attacked
And retreated down Wolf Creek
Warriors breathing down their backs

And rejoined their regiment
Where they met a grizzly scene
The blackened skeletons of lodge poles
Hot flames had lickened clean

Smoke engulfed the valley
Indian food and lodges . . . gone
The Arapaho would starve to death
With winter coming on

The soldiers took their ponies
At least eleven hundred head
Without his horse an Indian
Is about as good as dead

So they hounded Conner's soldiers
'til midnight, the sky was black
But no plunder was retaken
Nor no ponies taken back

The volunteers from Iowa
Escaped into the dark
One hundred ten miles they'd ridden
Since their camp on Piney Fork

Only just a handful of white men
Fell on the Tongue that day
While many red men died
Sixty or seventy that day

Eleven years later Custer's
Seventh Cavalry would lay foe
To Sitting Bull, Crazy Horse
And these Arapaho

On a summer's eve in August
You might hear the hooves of thunder
And the crack of Springfield rifles
In the meadow over yonder

You might hear the bugles blowin' charge
Then later on retreat
You might smell the smoke, see the flames
Or even feel the heat

You might see the Grande Encampment
A village on the Tongue
Two hundred fifty lodges
Where meat and sweet grass hung

You might even see Jim Bridger
With ten companies in blue
Or seven hundred Indians
Caught in battle, counting coups

On a summer's eve in August
You might hear the cannon roarin'
And the rattlin' sounds of sabers
And the Bugles on the mornin' . . .

Jean Mathisen-Haugen

Jean Mathisen-Haugen

An eighth generation descendant of a Lander Valley ranching family, Jean Mathisen was born in Riverton, Wyoming. An only child, she grew up in various towns around the cowboy state because her father was a highway patrolman. Her "growing-up years" were spent in the coal mining town of Kemmerer, where she attended elementary school at Diamondville, just south of the town where J. C. Penney established his first department store. She later attended high school in Lander and Riverton's Central Wyoming College.

The poet's ancestors, the Horneckers, date back to 1869 in Wyoming. Her great-great uncles arrived at the Miner's Delight gold camp on South Pass. Ernest and Matt Hornecker started the first ranches in the Lander Valley in 1872, along with John Borner, Calamity Jane's brother-law; and Jake Frey, who originated in the same small town in Germany.

Eight-year-old Jean wrote her first poem as a third grader in 1960, and has since published six books of poetry. Her first collection was produced when she was twelve, written for her ranching grandparents.

Her work has since been anthologized in some thirty chapbooks and *The Wyoming Rural Electric News* has featured her poetry for more than twenty years. She has also written more than five hundred articles about Wyoming and the West, as well as other topics. What motivates her to write? "An obsession and a passion to do so."

Jean says she writes "at least two poems a month or when I get an idea. My favorite is one I wrote about my father and I. It's called 'Dreamer's Rendezvous.' Eight members of her family also write, most of them cowboy poetry. She feels the genre is appealing to others because of it's "humor and the look at a wonderful way of life," although cowboy poetry could be improved, she said, "with better use of language and smoothing up rhymes."

One of her featured poems, "Cowboy Auction," is an example of cowboy humor. "Some folks actually thought I was going to an auction to bid on a cowboy," she said with a grin.

A member of Wyoming Writers, WyoPoets, Cowboy Poets of Idaho, and a charter member of Cowboy Poets of Wind River, she has performed at cowboy poetry gatherings in Wyoming, Idaho and Montana since 1988, including the Wyoming Centennial Celebration on the capitol grounds in Cheyenne in July 1990. A long-time member of Western Writers of America (WWA) and the Wyoming Association of Professional Historians, she's a past president of Wyoming Writers, Inc., and a three-time past president of WyoPoets.

Jean lived with her husband Ron in Lander, where she was once employed as a museum curator, and retired as an administrative specialist from the Wyoming Department of Transportation in 2003. In her spare time, she performs as a singer, accompanying herself on guitar and mandolin, and has written more than two dozen songs.

She and fellow Lander poet Verlin Pitt filed for a county commissioner's post in the 2004 election, both on the Republican ticket. To garner campaign funds, they jointly held a mini cowboy poetry gathering in their local park, where they combined verse with politics.

HEAVEN'S REACHES

I walked around the old campground
and saw some rusty cans.
I then recalled the story
Grampaw told of one good man.
He was roughshod 'round the edges,
would fight both bear and snake;
helped Grampaw tail the cattle
and he answered to just Jake.
They trailed in far from Oregon
shorthorn cattle in those days
here to the Lander Valley.
The longhorns in other ways.
Now Jake would eat most anything
that Cookie would ever fix,
from beans and bacon to cowboy stew,
and bakin' powder biscuits were his picks.
He liked jackrabbit to poached deer
and loved dried apple pie
that Cookie made with relish,
adding in an occasional fly.
But what he loved most of all,
that sent him to Heaven's reaches,
was when he used his jackknife
to pry open a can of peaches.

He figured manna from Heaven
that was mentioned in the Good Book
came in those old tin cans
and had the peaches' look.
Grampaw and Jake were good pals
and they'd made it across Idaho.
It was coming into fall now
and they were worried some about snow.
They were tailing down Green River
when the lightning began to flash
and the streaks were dancing on the cattle's horns
and the cattle started to dash.
The chuck wagon was caught in the middle
and the cattle were headed that way.
Looked like the wagon and Cookie were doomed,
but Jake did more than pray.
Grampaw yelled at him to hold back,
but Jake just plowed on in.
He was bound to save the wagon
and the last seen of him was a grin.
The stampede ended quickly
as a cloud passing over the moon.
The scene left behind was a bad one,
but the boys found Jake fairly soon.
The wagon and Cookie were safe now,
but a bull had gored old Jake,
taken his favorite horse down,
but he explained what he'd done was for their sake;

"Bury me on the hill, boys,
this campground will do just fine.
I have lived me a good life
and I think it was just my time.
I just had to save the wagon,
Ole Cookie and his tin wash tub,
for they were our necessities.
And most of all, we needed our grub.
And I hope the Lord will be kind to me
if I get to Heaven's Reaches
and let me have some jackrabbit stew
and a can of heavenly peaches!"
Jake's grave is not marked here
except by a pile of rusty tin cans
once full of the fruit that cowboy loved–
they were left for that brave man.
Grampaw settled in the valley here,
made a ranch and raised shorthorns.
Raised some kids and told each and every one
from the time that they were born
they'd best appreciate food to eat,
and if they wanted to taste Heaven's Reaches,
just get a can of something good–
but make darn sure it was peaches!

COWBOY AUCTION

We went to Bill's cowboy auction—
they had saddles, guns and spurs,
hamburgers, hotdogs and horses
and mitts made out of fur.
They had paintings and horse collars,
handcuffs, moccasins and a fiddle.
The auctioneer was there warming up his voice—
you could see him out there in the middle.
Now, Ma, she liked the buckskin mare
and a rifle took my eye,
but what I went to the auction for
they didn't have there to buy.
They called it a "cowboy auction"
but not a one of them was for sale.
Mustaches and chaw and scuffed-up boots—
they'd take one look and turn tail.
I call it false advertising,
calling that auction by that name.
By golly, I wanted a cowboy,
not a boot or a spur or a hame.
I got a bone to pick with you , Jones,
your advertising just ain't true—
if I can't get me a cowboy there,
then what's a poor girl to do?
You called this the first annual auction—
well, if you're gonna have another,
you'd best get a cowboy to sell to me
And another buckskin for my mother!

Kent Stockton, M. D.

Kent Stockton, M.D.

Throughout his early years, Kent Stockton's dream was to live the life of a cowboy. He said, "I was one of the few at Dartmouth College to wear underslung high-top boots and jeans." The Kansas City native fulfilled his dream by establishing a family medical practice in Riverton, Wyoming, some thirty years ago. He also became a rancher.

The doctor raises longhorn cattle, which pasture during the summer months near Dubois, Wyoming. "In the late fall we graze them on our alfalfa stubble here at home, and then from about January until June, I feed them in our corrals. We raise a few quarter horses to get the cow work done and to take pack trips in the summer and fall. I also do some day work for rancher friends."

Stockton's first poem was titled for one of his college professors. "Ode to Dr. Ekblaw." was composed in Ekblaw's earth science class at the university where the medical student met and fell in love with Mary Margaret, his wife of nearly forty years. "Dr. Ekblaw was the catalyst that brought us together."

Not long after the young couple moved to Wyoming in 1973, Dr. Stockton began taking part in team roping and wrote his first cowboy poem, although "at the time I didn't know there was such a thing as cowboy poetry."

The poem was titled "The Golden Rope," because "my first catch rope cost about ten bucks, but subsequent 'necessary' purchases escalated the cost of that rope substantially."

Stockton attended the 1987 Elko, Nevada, Cowboy Poetry Gathering and was "mighty enthused." He returned to start the Wyoming Cowboy Poetry Roundup that year, which continued annually in October until 1999. The doctor has also recited his poems at the Montana Cowboy Poetry Gathering and at Rapid City, South Dakota, as well as Fremont County, Wyoming.

He writes sporadically. "Every once in a while a theme, or an event, or a thought will grab me and I'll mull it over for a few weeks, maybe just a few days. Then I'll sit down and write it up in verse." It might take as little as an hour or he may set the poem aside and read it later, making a few changes. "But I don't feel any compulsion or pressure to turn out poetry. . . unless there's a good reason to. I just gotta go when the spirit hits me."

The doctor has been published in *The Western Horseman, Cowboy Magazine, Dry Crik Review, Range Magazine*, and *Bugle Magazine*. His poetry has also been included in two anthologies. He lists Badger Clark, Gail Gardner, Wally McRae and Gary McMahan among his favorite cowboy poets, and has memorized more "Bruce Kiskaddon poems than anyone else's."

His son Ty occasionally writes cowboy poetry while serving as the outdoor editor for the *Cheyenne Eagle-Tribune*. The elder Stockton feels that people enjoy the genre "because of several factors. It rhymes, it meters along almost like a song, and it tells of simple truths, hardships, and pleasures. It harks back to a less-complicated lifestyle, and one we're still privileged to enjoy in the rural West. I don't really know who reads it, but people who don't are usually pleasantly surprised when they do."

His featured poems are "The Houlihan" and "The Long Shadow Time."

The Houlihan

To rope a steer by head or heel
Ain't really all that tough,
An' snarlin' calves ain't no big deal
If you've done it long enough.

But there's a loop the cowboys know
That I can't understand–
That cayuse-snaggin' noose they throw
That's called the houlihan.

It's a quiet an' a gentle loop
That's thrown from way down low;
No whirlin' swing or screamin' whoop
Accompanies this throw.

It's like poetry as it flies,
But I can't find the combination
Regardless how I try.

I throw a rope with my left hand;
An' practice though I might,
When friends show me the houlihan
They throw it with their right.

They demonstrate artistic line–
It's simple, smooth an' neat–
Then I'll try, an' soon my twine
Is piled up at my feet.

I've practiced til my arm is sore
But that throw's beyond my scope.
The dogs don't even run no more
When they see me with my rope.

To make a hand's my fondest dream
But if I may be candid,
That houlihan ain't in my scheme–
It cain't be throwed left-handed.

The Long Shadow Time

Those moments just before the dusk
Inspire a man to rhyme—
The favorite time for all of us
Is the day's Long Shadows Time.

For the greens are never greener
Nor clearer the coyotes's bark;
The details never cleaner
Than in the magic just 'fore dark.

'Tis then a peaceful calm descends;
The winds are put on hold.
A vivid, oblique light transcends
The now, the new, the old—

The critters seem to feel it, too;
That's when they most aspire
To join in nature's vast milieu,
Just 'fore the sun retires.

The melody of meadowlark,
The crow of rooster pheasant
Are clearest just before the dark,
And infinitely more pleasant.

Sit quiet on your favorite bay
Or on your pasture fence
An' view the earth at end o' day—
'Twas never more immense.

The moments after sunrise
Are nearly as sublime—
But they can't hold a candle
To the day's Long Shadows Time.

Echo Roy-Klaproth

Echo Roy-Klaproth

The poet grew up on a cattle and sheep ranch between Douglas and Gillette, Wyoming, "sixty miles from any where." Echo had three brothers, all members of a fourth generation ranching family. Although the youngest brother "was lost in 1990 to cancer, the survivors remain active in ranching and farming," she said. Her oldest brother, Jerry, runs the family ranch–"what we refer to as the headquarters"–and Floyd ranches south of Douglas with his in-laws, and keeps our farm going."

Echo serves as bookkeeper and takes care of the business end of ranching. "We consider it a privilege to be members of the fourth generation on Wyoming soil and so all three of us work to maintain the legacy we were handed at birth."

The mother of three lost one son, Travis, in 2003 to cancer, but counts her blessings that he left behind two sons to "keep his memory alive." Another son, Tye, lives in Laurel, Montana, with his wife Shelley and two children, and her daughter Amanda is working on a college degree while raising her own young daughter.

Echo Roy met her present husband Rick at a cowboy poetry gathering in Riverton during October of 1991. "He shares my love of Wyoming, country life, family values, and the belief that the most important things in life are gifts from God. He's my biggest fan and supporter, and a most faithful partner in life."

She left the family ranch during the late 1980s and moved to Fremont County where she served as a newspaper journalist for *The Wrangler Horse and Rodeo News* in Riverton for ten years. "I loved every aspect of that job, however, there were no opportunities for advancement. So at age 45, I went back to college and got a degree in teaching."

Majoring in English, she decided to teach creative writing at the community college level, but the first job opportunity to present itself was six miles from home at Shoshoni High School, where she's been teaching seventh through twelfth grade English and Yearbook ever since, "and loving every minute of it."

The ranch girl was introduced to poetry at age eight. Her first grade teacher, Mrs. Evans, taught her a love of poetry and helped her memorize Rudyard Kipling's "If" poem, "which won me a grand prize at our 4-H talent show. I wrote to save our heritage, keep our stories alive for our children and their children. Later, I began writing poetry as a way to help me survive a divorce. I only discovered in the mid-1980s that what I wrote was called cowboy poetry because it represented a specific lifestyle."

A friend accompanied her to Cody, Wyoming, in 1987, to her first cowboy poetry gathering, and "I was hooked for life. I loved hearing the stories—our stories—told in rhyme, meter or song." A year later, she recited her own poetry at the Bar J in Jackson, Wyoming, at the urging of a friend, Bob Loper. Since that time, she has been traveling the region performing and sharing her poetry. "Of all my experiences," she said, "the three biggest thrills to date have been the night show at the Cowboy Poetry Gathering in Riverton in 1990, representing Wyoming at the national gatherings in Elko, Nevada; and performing at the Smithsonian's Wolf Trap Theater in Washington, D. C. in 1995 on a ranch radio program."

Life, she said, motivates her to write. "I've had poems wake me up in the night. They won't leave me alone. I've had poems come to me in a crowd, so I jot down a few lines on whatever's handy so I don't lose the thought. I get many ideas for writing while I'm driving or on the rare occasions that I get horseback these days. If I'm alone, my mind can wander at leisure and I just follow along, trying to capture the words when they come."

"Branding Day" and "A Ride Across the Pasture" are examples of Echo Roy-Klaproth's creative wanderings.

Branding Day

As the sun peeks up over the hill
A meadowlark greets and the brandin' fire heats
While we shake off the mornin' chill.
Steam rolls from the cups that we hold
And the day comes alive as neighbors arrive
In tradition that's treasured and old.

Vaccine's bein' loaded in the guns,
Ropes are shook and knives put to use
As the crew goes to work, unison.
Ropers drag their prize through the bunch
Amid laughter and blood, confusion and mud
In a rhythm gaining speed before lunch.

Smoke curls toward the clear mornin' blue
When the hot iron sears markin' heifer and steer
While each momma bawls her fear anew.
It's the young and the old side by side
As wrestlin' becomes play, the sweat rolls way
In an outline all taken in stride.

It's an age old custom held fast
And one that will cost if ever it's lost
Cause brandin' day's part of our past,
There's more than a job needin' done.
It's a family pride and friendships besides
Tyin' the old to the new, and as one.

A Ride Across the Pasture

As I ride across the pasture
With its smells of sage and hay
I find my mind is a wanderin'
Imagin' how it was in older days.

It's hard to picture this land here
Without the progress and its consequences.
God, I bet it was grand to top a rise
Seeing uncluttered miles with no fences.

I've heard the grass used to be taller
And water ran clear in the creek.
You could ride for miles without a stop
And not see a neighbor for a week.

I'm sure the sounds were more comfortin'
A breeze whisperin' by or a cow a' bawlin',
Instead of a truck roarin' away
Or a pump jack up the draw a' squallin'.

While knowing I'm luckier than most,
Cause I'm riding' across this pasture
Lookin' for a picture that's lost.

John Nesbitt

John Nesbitt

John Nesbitt's western poetry often places him outside the traditional cowboy poetry form, because some of his poems don't rhyme and he doesn't have them memorized. He enjoys the work of Mark Todd and Laurie Wagner Buyer as well as gatherings that are "less dogmatic about poetry." He especially likes to take part in events that feature western singers and songwriters such as Mike Blakely, Jon Chandler, W. C. Jameson, and Wyoming's Kevin McNiven.

John's own first cowboy poem, "You are the Pearl of My Mountain Oyster" had been "kicking around" in his head "and needed to get out." Published in one of his short stories in *West Wind Review,* it received the best short story award and was reprinted in his collection, *Antelope Sky.*

An instructor of English and Spanish at Eastern Wyoming College in Torrington, he has participated in the Cheyenne Cowboy Symposium as well as group and solo readings.

"Because I have a full-time teaching job, I write whenever I can find time in the evening, on weekends, and during breaks.

"I believe that I have something to express about life, and I feel compelled to express it in writing. I'm also motivated by the desire to be successful as a writer—that is, to get published and have readers." Ian Tyson is his favorite cowboy poet because "he expresses true northern spirit and does not deal in trite treatments."

The poet has been published in several areas. His literary articles and book reviews have appeared in *Western American Literature, South Dakota Review, Journal of the West*, and other journals. His fiction, nonfiction and poetry have been published in numerous literary magazines, including *Wyoming: The Hub of the Wheel, The Dakotah, Owen Wister Review*, and *West Wind Review*. They have also appeared in *Roundup Magazine*, and several Wyoming Writers, Inc. publications.

The author has nine traditional western novels to his credit, including *One-Eyed Cowboy Wild, Coyote Trail, For the Norden Boys*, and *Black Hat Butte* as well as two contemporary western novels: *Keep the Wind in Your Face* and *A good Man to Have in Camp*.

His writings also include his doctoral dissertation, a textbook for basic writing courses, manuals for composition and literature courses as well as a booklet about Robert Roripaugh, a former Wyoming poet laureate.

He is most proud of his long narrative poem, "When My Pony Sheds Again," a fun poem, he said, to read aloud. Although the work is over 200 lines, it appears in Adventures of the Ramrod Rider, a medley of fiction, poetry, satire and parody.

"Readers love the cowboy poetry genre because it is simple and direct," he said. "It often speaks to the reader's experience and reaffirms the reader's values. People like it because it rhymes, because it is not highly intellectual– and is often anti-intellectual– because it is often sentimental, and because it often contains clean humor. Another way of saying it is that people like cowboy poetry because it is safe."

His poem/song, "Please Come to Wyoming," appears in his western novel, *Black Hat Butte*, and is featured here, as is "Nebraska Girl," which can be found in another of his novels, *For the Norden Boys*.

Please Come to Wyoming

Out on the wide prairie in broad sunny grasslands,
Or back in a canyon 'midst cottonwood trees,
Wherever the wildflowers bloom in the springtime,
You'll hear this sweet song on the soft evening breeze:

Yoodle-ooh, yoodle-ooh-hoo, so sings a lone cowboy,
who with the wild roses wants you to be free.

This hand that I offer is yours now and always,
Please take it, my darling, step into the light;
The darkness and clouds you can leave there behind you,
As forward you move into fields warm and bright.

I offer you sunshine and flowers, my darling,
A few simple things from a country boy's world,
Please come to my arms now and let me protect you,
Please come to Wyoming, to sunlight and me.

Out on the wide prairie in broad sunny grasslands,
Or back in a canyon 'midst cottonwood trees,
Wherever the wildflowers bloom in the springtime,
You'll hear this sweet song on the soft evening breeze.

Yoodle-ooh, yoodle-ooh-hoo, so sings a lone cowboy,
who with the wild roses wants you to be free.

Nebraska Girl

I've got a girl back in Nebraska
With sparking eyes and long, dark hair—
A voice that rings with golden laughter,
And lips that brush away all care.

When last I saw her in Nebraska,
Beneath the spring-time moon so bright,
She whispered words demure and tender,
And held me in her arms so tight.

The golden moon above Nebraska
Lit up the prairie with its glow—
And showed to me a scene of wonder,
A dark-haired goddess here below.

I had to leave her in Nebraska—
But I'll go back when roundup's done,
And meet her on the golden prairie
Beneath the smiling autumn sun.

And when the winter in Nebraska
Gives way to prairie flowers in bloom,
We'll walk together, slow at sunset,
And watch the rising of the moon.

And when the moon above Nebraska
Lights up the evening warm and free,
We'll pledge our love in moonlit whispers,
My sweet Nebraska girl and me.

Ada McDonell

Ada McDonell

Ada Maxine Gustin was born in an old clapboard house three miles south of Ethete, Wyoming, on the Wind River Indian Reservation, the youngest of five children. "After I was born, my mother had to take care of the livestock on horseback and she would put me in a flour sack that hung from the saddle horn," she said.

Her father was elected to the school board when Ada was five, and she and her siblings attended a one-room school with Arapaho children. "We had to ride horses to school and pack our lunch in a syrup bucket." During winter, the schoolhouse was so cold that "our sandwiches were frozen and it sounded like you were eating ground glass."

Ada wrote her first poem about a horse, which was published in *WREN Magazine* during the late 1970s. "From then on, writing and poetry kept sneaking into my brain and I enjoyed writing about things that have happened to me and the animals we owned and encountered."

When Kent Stockton established the Wyoming Cowboy Poetry Gathering, she was asked to recite some of her work. "Boy, was I scared when it came my turn, those hot lights glaring down." She was then asked to perform at the Elko, Nevada, gathering, but was unfortunately unable to attend.

Many of her poetry ideas stem from her cowhand's job on a large ranch in Montana. She said, "I was the only woman who got to ride with the guys." The saddest poem she wrote was about her aunt, who died as an infant and was buried in the Rattlesnake Mountains. "This one made some of the ladies in the audience cry," she said, "and I have a hard time reading it."

Like "the old-timers, I use their language and their sayings which some of the younger generation can't understand. Baxter Black is a great poet for cowboy lingo and has a way of expressing himself that us older people have heard all our lives. The other [poet] that I admire is an old cowboy by the name of Nate Brown. Nate is a real hand with horses and enjoys what he does. His horses turn out well broke, too."

The poet's research also stems from driving tractor, gathering and checking cattle, feeding a thousand head of sheep every morning at four, and breaking horses to ride. She worked at her family's dude ranch in the Wind River Mountains, learned to pack horses for the hunt, "and saw a lot of beautiful country."

Her talents include oil painting. A number of them have sold "for a pretty fair price." Her favorite painting is of two Angus bulls fighting, which she regrets selling. However, the "Mean Old Cow" she wrote about here was not a bovine she would hesitate to sell.

Mean Old Cow

Came upon this old cow,
She was bogged down in the mud,
It seemed she hit it a running,
And it stopped her with a thud.
Eyes wild and bulging,
She lay there in the bog.
The way she fought that mud,
She reminded me of a hog.

I waded out to where she lay,
She eyed me with all fear.
Put the loop under her head,
By grabbing a muddy ear.
She blew snot in my face,
And bellered loud and mean.
Old Mighty stood upon the bank,
A taken in the scene.

Took my dallies on the horn,
And Old Mighty pulled the slack.
The leather creaked, and Mighty strained,
To free that bony rack.
The old cow how she struggled,
She gave it all she had.
Her neck stretched, her eyes rolled,
And things were looking pretty bad.

Finally with a forceful tug,
The one that did the trick,
And she came a sliding,
Right into the creek.
Went up to her muddy head,
My rope to retrieve.
And as my hand pulled on the rope,
To take it from her neck.
She gained her feet and ran me down,
And stomped me in the creek.

I called her every dirty name,
That I have ever thought.
Thank God for Old Mighty
For he still had her caught.
She fought the rope and wrung her tail,
And tried to gore my horse.
But Old Mighty he out danced
That ornery cow, of course.

Finally got on Mighty,
back in my leather throne,
She hits the rope a running,
And my horse he gave a groan.
Maybe she'll have a heart attack,
And this I kind of hope
Thinking that's the only way
I might regain my rope.

Old Mighty he keeps working,
As the sweat shows on his hide.
I finally get my bearings,
And we give that cow a ride.
Dragging and a bellering,
Now this may calm her pride.
Her eyes are shut, her tongue is out,
And she's heaving in the sides.
Finally settles down some,
And I decide to try again.
But this old gal is bound and determined,
That she is going to win.

I fly into the saddle,
As her horns just graze my rear.
If I had my rifle,
I'd shoot her in the ear.
Maybe if I cut the rope,
And let this old beast loose,
With some luck an eastern hunter,
Will kill her for a moose.

Around and around we go,
Until we three are spent.
She slowly goes to her knees,
As if she will repent.
I see my chance to bail off,
And finally get my twine.
I ride away into the blue,
From that mean old cow of mine.

Ron Bailey

Ron Bailey

A fifth generation rancher-cowboy, Ron Bailey was the second of three sons born to a South Dakota family. Following one semester of college, he married and managed to buy a ranch of his own. After a number of years, however, "We fell on hard times and sold out to avoid going broke in 1982."

The Baileys moved to Wyoming, where they found "real jobs," and continued to raise and train Quarter Horses on a small ranch west of Riverton. Bailey retired from his custodial job with the school district in June 2004, with plans to pursue his "vices of hunting, fishing and riding around in the mountains" as well as writing cowboy poetry.

His first poem was written for his wife Lorri for their twenty-fifth wedding anniversary. He wrote his first cowboy poem three weeks following the death of his father in 1991. "The words just started falling out of my head so fast I couldn't hardly write them down fast enough," he said." I entitled it simply "Dad" and it can be found in my first book of cowboy poetry, *Horses I Have Known (And Some I wish I Hadn't)*." His second book was published two years later, titled, *Horses, Friends and Good Times*.

Bailey performs in cowboy poetry gatherings in his own area as well as surrounding states. He also performs solo for various organizations as well as private readings, but doesn't confine his writing to poetry. He has also written about two horseback pack trips to Wyoming wilderness areas, which were published in *Western Horseman Magazine*.

Although his poetry is mainly serious, Bailey recalls a humorous incident during the summer of 1993 while he was performing cowboy poetry every Friday evening for the guests at a Jackson Hole dude ranch. As he stood greeting the guests arriving for the performance, he tipped his hat "as a good cowboy and gentleman should to one of the ladies, and her husband wanted to know why I had saluted his wife instead of him."

He considers "Abandoned Ranch" his best poem because "it contains the very essence of the struggles and joys of the ranch business and the fact that everything contained in it has happened to me or some past member of my family."

Abandoned Ranch

I rode slowly over the hill,
There on the creek flats below,
Stood an old abandoned ranch,
You've all seen them, I know.

Standing out there on the prairie,
Or maybe back up in some draw,
The old corral's now falling down,
The barn door and open maw.

I sat there and thought a while,
This one seemed special to me,
It looked like one my ancestors
had ranched on, don't you see.

I thought of the work needed,
Just to build that first shack.
Something to barely live in,
With an outhouse in the back.

Then to send for the family,
And with them keep working hard,
Trying to get the barn built,
By the house a little yard.

The yard, barbed wire fence,
Just to keep the cattle out,
To protect a tree and flowers,
And the wash they hung out

Carry water up from the creek,
'Till they could dig a well,
The backbreaking work they did,
I can never begin to tell.

So many things done by hand,
Digging post hole and chopping wood,
Working from dawn 'till after dark,
Resting and playing when they could.

Playing cards or some parlor game,
By the flicker of kerosene light,
Or maybe sometimes a big dance,
That lasted all through the night.

Horse racing and baseball games,
Played on the Fourth of July,
With that kind of busy life,
The years really do go by.

Can you see the new house,
Hear the sound of children's feet,
Happy laughter out on the porch,
On holidays the family would meet.

Sitting down to a big meal,
Sharing whatever they had,
Talking about last year's crops,
Sharing the good and the bad.

After supper sitting on the porch,
Talking about the weather and such,
Hoping for a good calf crop,
The prices going up a touch.

The finances of such a place,
Always a squeeze at very best,
Seemed like there was always something,
Coming along, giving 'em another test.

Always hard times and endless work,
Maybe husband or wife dying,
But work still must be done,
And not much time for crying.

Then there was always the weather,
Both their enemy and their friend,
Sometimes dry and sometimes wet,
And the wind blowing without end.

Down through a couple of generations,
Passing it on or just starting new,
Sometimes working the ranch alone,
And sometimes maybe hiring a crew.

There were truly men and women,
Running the ranches of this land,
Eventually getting modern tools,
Not doing so much by hand.

So why are these ranches abandoned,
Reduced to the rubble we see,
Standing there empty and so lonely,
Causing memories for you and me.

Some were passed on for a while,
Down to a daughter or son,
To carry on as best they could,
With this land so hard won.

Then along came the big depression,
Drought and many a place was lost,
Low prices and overdue mortgage,
Many could not afford the cost.

Some were lost for the taxes,
They just couldn't afford to pay,
Later someone else bought the land,
And maybe still owns it today.

Some managed to somehow hang on,
Doing everything they could do,
But just had no one left,
They could pass it on to.

Got old and retired to town,
And to the neighbor did sell,
Though it makes them so sad.
This story they now must tell.

The neighbor, his own home place,
And the buildings just didn't need,
And so now as we can see,
The place has gone to weed.

No matter what has caused it,
No one lives there anymore,
On those ranches we see empty,
And no matter what happened before.

All that are left are the memories,
And I guess that they must do,
So that we will always remember,
What it means to me and you.

So when one of these places,
Out there you happen to see,
Think of the place you grew up,
And how it may someday be.

We can't see into the future,
To know what will happen someday,
But like those abandoned ranches,
We'll also be lonesome some day.

Your children will have their memories,
So this should be your plan,
Try to make those memories good,
Always do the best you can.

Gene Shea

Gene Shea

Hanna, Wyoming, poet Gene Shea was "raised on a dry land cattle and grain farm in Kansas" during the dust bowl years of the 1930s. "Most kids were lucky to have completed high school, so a few workshops, seminars and special courses are all the college I have," he said. His high school education was enough to pave the way for his small securities brokerage firm in Rawlins, from which he retired.

He remembers entertaining himself as a child "making up rhymes in a one-room school" with two younger brothers and a sister. He wrote his first cowboy poem during the early 1970s. "I wrote a little poetry just for the fun of it after I finished the manuscript for a novel that never flew," he said. The poem was later included in his first self published chap book, *Antidote for Cabin Fever*, released in 1993.

Cowboy poetry has always been popular in small towns and rural areas of the West, where it's a way of life, he said. "The hippie movement and beatnik poetry of the sixties and seventies drove the great national poetry audience away from conventional poetry when it was taken over by the garbage that passed for poetry at that time. A lot of those readers are now coming back to cowboy poetry—especially the older readers—as it's the closest thing to what they were raised on as children, just learning and establishing an opinion about poetry."

A past president of WyoPoets, he was Wyoming's delegate to the NFSPS national conventions in 2002 and 2003. He has also served as contest director for Wyoming's nationwide poetry contest five of the past six years and frequently judges poetry contests in various parts of the nation.

Gene Shea writes both cowboy and conventional poetry, "most of it in cowboy style," some 1,100 published poems over the years. His seven books include *Antidote to Cabin Fever, When the Magpie Sings, Crossbar Hotel, Barefoot in the Briars, Birds of a Feather, Windfall Watermelons,* and *Duck Soup.*

His poems, "Medicine Bow River" and "Snow Shovel Epitaph" are featured here.

Medicine Bow River

Old river that heads in the highlands
In the Land of the Midsummer Snow,
Above the line of the timbered lands,
Above where the last scrub pine stands,
Bonsaied by the Arctic winds that blow.

There, on the thin spine of the world
That parts the waters of East and West,
Where snow clouds come unfurled,
Where worst of winter's blizzards swirled,
With breath of spring is eventually blessed.

Side of the mountain first touched by sun
Creeps a tiny trickle of molten snow,
Following this path since time begun,
Meeting where other rivulets run,
To emerge as a tumbling brook below.

Ice cold and clear as a crystal light,
Birthed and fed by the mountain snow,
Gathering siblings from left and right,
Down from the mountains in its flight,
Splash the icy waters of the Medicine Bow.

Plunge from the mountains to valley below
Where man takes over and has the say,
Where cattle is king and hay crops grow
Where water is short, they lack the snow,
Find her waters diverted to raising of hay.

What water is left, to the desert must go
Where alkali and the mud flats bake
No resemblance now to the ice and snow
For only a tepid trickle will flow
To merge with the waters of Seminoe Lake.

Valley meadows grow tall and wave in the wind,
Cattle winter well on the timothy hay.
Thus are the cycles of both rivers and men
Few amount to much when we reach the end.
Please search for the good we did along the way.

Snow Shovel Epitaph

So much snow I shovel in Wyoming
And I've shoveled it all my life,
I might mistake a snow shovel
And think I took it for a wife.

Nine months of every year
and sometimes ten or more,
I bust my butt at shoveling
 To keep the snowdrift from my door.

When I die and they bury me
On the hill out south of town
Please, take my shovel along
And set the handle in the ground.

And on it scribe my epitaph,
To all this wide world tell,
"He wasn't much as a poet,
 But he shoveled snow quite well."

Leslie Keltner

Leslie Keltner

Leslie Keltner not only writes and performs cowboy poetry, she composes her own songs and accompanies herself on the guitar and washtub bass, which consists of a galvanized tub, shovel handle, and cotton clothesline. The washtub bass is "quite simple," she said, "and makes a great rhythm instrument." An accomplished singer, her voice has been compared to that of the late Patsy Cline.

The former ranch girl owns a consignment clothing store in Cody. Born in Halliday, North Dakota, the youngest of seven children, she attended college for one year and says, "I'm continuing my education on a daily basis in the good old school of life as we know it."

When Leslie is not tending her store or traveling to perform cowboy poetry and music, she occasionally serves as a wilderness hunting camp cook. Her husband cowboyed until five years ago and now builds log homes and serves as a farrier. The couple also helps neighbors "when there's cattle work to be done."

The mother of two daughters began writing and performing cowboy poetry in 1990, but said she has always written poems. After attending the Cowboy Songs and Range Ballads performance in Cody, she went home thinking she could perform as well. She published a cassette of her work in 1993, and began work on a CD "to be produced as time, money and ambition will allow."

Leslie has performed at weddings, funerals, barbeques, rodeos, churches, bars, chuck wagon cookouts, brandings, trail rides, and cattle drives as well as nursing homes, banquets, sorority meetings, dude ranches, chambers of commerce meetings, family reunions, hunting camps and "the top of Deer Creek Pass." Her travels have taken her to Colorado, Nebraska, North Dakota, Montana, Idaho, and various towns in Wyoming.

"I consider it an honor every time I take the stage, because people are taking the time to listen to me." The poet writes whenever the mood strikes. "Sometimes it's a random thought that develops into an entire poem in seemingly an instant, and sometimes it's a thought that has been brewing for ages and eventually comes bubbling out.

"I'm most motivated by human behavior and everyday occurrences. My family and friends are constant sources," she said, "and sometimes it's my vivid imagination that gets carried away."

Elizabeth Ebert of Thunder Hawk, South Dakota, is her favorite poet. "She is to me the grande dame of cowboy poetry. She touches the souls of people, both with her humor and sincerity." Leslie feels that people relate to cowboy poetry for two reasons. "Some enjoy it because they, too, are living our lifestyle, and the others because they wish they could live like us. I can say that because of my poetry, I've met people from literally around the world, many of whom I now call 'friend.' Every gathering has become like a family reunion—complete with a few weird uncles—where everyone is there to enjoy themselves."

Leslie Keltner was introduced at a Montana gathering by someone she had known for years. "She said she didn't know anybody who has as much fun as I do. I believe that life is far too short to be unhappy, and I take full advantage of everything life offers me. I hope people will remember my laughter, my smile, and that I was always willing to lend a hand."

Her featured poem, "The Price of a Horse," could be subtitled "Poetic Justice."

The Price of a Horse

"It's just a horse," he'd tell her,
"And you know he's past his prime.
Heck, canner price is fifty cents,
he's got to go this time."
She'd look at him with tear-filled eyes
and vigorously shake her head.
"No," she'd say, "I'll find another way
to pay the bills instead."
He'd scoff at her, slam the door,
and head out to the bar.
She'd sit and suffer silently,
wondering how she'd got in this far.
Her friends and family had said
he'd only bring her down,
but she'd fiercely held on to him,
although they pitied her in town.
She's smart and a pretty girl,"
they'd shake their heads and say.
No one knew what she saw in him,
even to this day.
She was a dedicated hard worker,
honest as the day is long.
He was commonly known as a rounder,
never held a job too long.
The little they had was because of her,
all paid for by her, on time.
The little he made, when he bothered to work,
he drank up, down to the last dime.

And every time things started looking rough,
he'd threaten to sell her horse,
'cause according to him, it cost too much
to support her habit, of course.
But she'd had that horse for twenty-four years,
and you just don't sell a friend.
She'd made a silent promise
that she'd keep him to the end.
There were days he didn't look the best,
so she'd give him extra grain,
and stand by him, and whisper,
an softly stroke his mane.
They'd been through so much together,
the miles and the years.
He was the only one she talked to;
he'd heard all her dreams and fears.
There was no way she'd ever sell him,
she'd starve herself that he'd have hay,
'cause that's just what you do,
when you love something that way.
"Horse sale this coming Saturday;
fifty-cents is canner price.
We could pay off a bill or two,
maybe get you something nice."
She'd look at him with love-gone eyes,
now filled with only hate,
shake her head and wonder
how she'd picked him for a mate.
That morning came when she awoke,
her heart hammering with dread.
What sound had just awakened her,
as she lifted up her head?

She heard the slam of the corral gate,
and whinny of old Blue,
and in an instant, without a doubt,
she knew what she must do.
So quickly grabbing boots and jeans
she headed out for the pen;
grabbed the 30-30 as she went by
and jacked a bullet in.
He half-smiled as he saw her,
and tried to make amends;
still drunk from a night at the bar
in town with friends.
"Aw, hon, now don't tell me
that you'd rather put him down
than get fifty-four cents canner price
at the sale today in town."
She hit him right between the eyes,
and he dropped like an old grain sack.
She never even broke her stride
and she didn't bother looking back.
She jerked the halter off of Blue,
and calmed him with some grain;
went inside and called the sheriff;
said she really couldn't explain
what had happened here this morning
and she didn't know what to do,
'cause her husband had just shot himself
when he went to kill old Blue.
"I begged him not to do it,
'cause he was drunk and could get hurt,
but he said it needed doing,
and now he's out there in the dirt.

I guess he must have stumbled
and pulled the trigger as he went down.
I think he's dead but would you please
send an ambulance from town?"
There wasn't much to say;
tragic accidents happen, you know?
Her family and friends brought pies and cakes
to help her ease her sorrow.
Old Blue greets her every morning,
They both know his day is coming,
but they'll leave it up to fate.
She'll never more go hungry, and there's
always grain and hay,
'cause double indemnity life insurance
was the bill she always made sure to pay.

Verlin Pitt

Verlin Pitt

Cowboy poetry is loved by both readers and audiences alike because "the American West is our heritage," according to Verlin Pitt, a Fremont County deputy sheriff. "Cowboy poetry spans the continent, and the humor and values of the American people are reflected in it. I suspect that just about everyone has read a little cowboy poetry."

Robert Service is his favorite poet and his own poetry has earned praise from fellow writers of western verse. His poems began at the age of 15, and he said that anything that walks, crawls, talks or bucks motivates him to write. As a teen, he wrote about gunfighters, cowboys, Indians, western towns and events, "which is pretty much what I write about today." His interests as a youngster varied from riding horses to roaming the creeks and rivers in the Lander area. He also rode bareback broncs in a few rodeos but decided not to follow the circuit. "I grew up around old-timers who spent their lives on ranches in the West," who as a result, "had a good sense of humor."

His creative talents as a youngster included working with leather, a sideline he still pursues. "Somewhere along the line I developed an interest in building lodgepole furniture and I've sold quite a few pieces." He also likes to draw, especially cartoons. But cowboy poetry is his first love. "I was thinking about a poem when my mustang mare bucked off the saddle with me in it," he said smiling. "Horses have ESP."

Verlin didn't intend to make law enforcement his career. It just happened. "In fact, in my younger years, I was probably one of the reasons law enforcement is needed. I was what you might call a problem cowboy. I went into law enforcement in my forties when I applied for a deputy sheriff's job, and darned if I didn't get hired. Now that I think about it, I have to wonder if they just wanted me where they could keep a closer eye on me."

Prior to law enforcement, he cowboyed on ranches, spent seventeen years in the oilfields, and served as a mine electrician. He also loaded bombs on merchant ships and worked as a cook, as well as "a few other things when I had to," he said. The deputy has been paid for some of his performances. "I like being paid, of course, but I do it out of a love for cowboy poetry." He began performing in a bar in Lander, "a pretty easy way to get started because no one seems to notice when you falter or make a mistake. At times they don't even seem to notice you're there."

His poem, "Silent Thunder" follows.

SILENT THUNDER

Like a Spring breeze they roam where they please,
a monarch of the prairie.
It's the freedom he feels, when he shows his heels,
he's wild and he's wary.
High on the plains, with their flowing manes,
wild horses sniff the air.
A big black stud lopes though the mud
and calls a buckskin mare.

Down through the years it's been a trail of tears
for those that had to tame one.
It takes a lot of force for a man to break a horse
under a blazing sun.
There are those that claim in a bid for fame,
they can break any horse with a back.
Rope and throw is what they know,
then cover the eyes with a sack.

When the cinch is tight, let 'em see the light
and buck that cayuse out. It's a darn good show,
but it's the hard way to go and a fool's route.
Using force to break will only make the bronc
learn to respond to force
I tell you, Pard, when you break 'em hard,
you take the spirit from the horse.

That are hurt from a club or quirt
are the hardest ones to tame.
The scars on their hide and the hurt inside
 ignite a burning flame.
The fire is fanned by the touch of a hand
and makes its mind go mad.
The hate inside from a real hard ride
can turn a good horse bad.

I'm here to say there's a better way
and I met a man who knows.
Paralyzed in a wreck below the neck
and yet his spirit flows.
Some men just quit when they're forced to sit
and watch the world go by.
These men will talk of a wish to walk,
but I know one that chose to fly.

Early on in life he faced some strife,
but it turned his life around.
His thoughts came clear on a horse's fear
and every thought was sound.
Stanford Addison was the chosen one,
when it came to taming horses.
Let the bronc unwind and it will find
it's facing unseen forces.

It soon comes clear there's magic here,
inside a horse corral.
From a bronc that's mean to a peaceful scene,
a bronc becomes a pal.
The spirit is saved and the road is paved
to create yourself a mount.
In a little while, you'll ride in style
on a horse that you can count.

Out in the West, there lives the best,
when it comes to breaking horses.
The Arapaho nation on the reservation
is where he teaches courses.
A quiet man with a gentle hand
and horse sense that is rare.
Some men claim they can do the same,
but can they do it from a wheelchair

Beneath a full moon drifts a haunting tune
that comes from a cedar flute.
The night joins in with its next of kind,
and echoes a hoot owl's hoot.
There is magic there in the prairie air
and it causes folks to wonder.
A bronc is fanned with a gentle hand
that drums out silent thunder.

Rick Pitt

Rick Pitt

Rick Pitt and his older brother Verlin have competed in events such as the Kanab, Utah, Cowboy Poetry Rodeo, where Rick took fifth place as a serious poet and Verlin placed third in the humor category.

"Verlin has been my best motivation to write. He's been doing it for many years and it's something we can participate in together as brothers. He made me read everything he wrote so I thought I'd make him read my scribblin' too."

Rick lists his brother as his favorite cowboy poet. Next in line is Gail Gardener, the author of "The Sierry Petes," written in 1917. "My dad used to recite a revised version of it to me when I was little."

The brothers were born in the Lander, Wyoming, area, with four brothers and two sisters. Rick attended one semester of college and secured a job at the Wyoming State Training School, where he has worked since 1982. The large facility encompasses forty buildings and is home to a hundred developmentally disabled residents, many of them confined to wheelchairs. "The facility was expanded to include units for traumatic brain injury victims as well as those with alcohol, drug and psychological problems."

Rick works in operations and assists the manager in "tasks too numerous to mention. I've done everything from repairing equipment to teaching classes to new staff members, to writing up budget requests. I never could figure out how they came up with my job title of trade specialist. I think 'Jack of all trades" would be more appropriate."

The poem of which he's most proud is "Angel of the West," written for his wife. "And I meant it more than any other. A lady once told me it's a poem every woman wants her man to write to her."

The poet was out one night with his wife when "someone hollered my name. A large man with long red hair in a ponytail and tie dyed T-shirt came up to me and asked if I was Rick Pitt, the cowboy poet. I was shocked but told him, yes, I was. He shook my hand and told me he read my stuff at cowboypoetry.com on the Internet and really enjoyed it. It's when I realized cowboys weren't the only ones reading this stuff."

His poems, "A Heck of a Ride" "Angel of the West," and "Dallas" follow next and have been enjoyed by many.

A Heck of a Ride

His clothes are old and dusty,
His hat is slightly torn.
He wears a scarf around his neck,
His boots are badly worn.

He used to be a bull rider,
He rode in all the fairs,
But now he's old and busted,
He can barely climb the stairs.

He used to be a fearless man,
He'd dog the meanest steer.
But that was then and this is now,
Today he just sips beer.

He wears the scars,
Of a thousand fights.
From drunken brawls,
Under bar room lights.

In years gone by,
It was widely known,
He was one cow hand,
You should leave alone.

His thoughts now drift,
To years long past.
A young girl's love,
That didn't last.

The dreams he had,
Have mostly died,
But he had to admit,
It was a heck of a ride.

Angel of the West

As I sit and try to ponder,
Why you've stayed by me so long.
I don't want to use another's words,
You've heard in some old song.

So I guess that I'll just say it,
If you hadn't took my hand.
I'd be livin' life for nothin',
In that place called no man's land.

All the troubles that I've suffered,
As I've tried to make my way.
You've been standin' there beside me.
With great patience I must say.

As we push on through the problems,
In this life that we must bare.
I know I could not endure as much,
Without your love and care.

You're the paint upon the canvas,
In a master work of art.
Without you to inspire me,
My dreams would fall apart.

I do thank the Lord above me,
For the day he gave me you.
If it weren't for his sweet kindness,
You could paint this cowboy blue.

Of all the things I've loved in life,
You're the lady I love best,
You're the good in my good-morning,
You're my angel of the West.

Dallas

I read a poem a while back,
It made me mad as . . . well.
Said we all had Texas in us,
Made this Wyoming cowboy yell.

I was born here in Wyoming,
And that's where I'm gonna stay.
I reckon I'll be buried here,
If I've anything to say.

Now those Texans might be darn good hands,
I really do not know.
Cause ya see I've never been there,
And I'll probably never go.

I hear they're mighty boastful,
That they like to brag a bit.
But I've heard some locals stretch the truth,
On nights that they got lit.

See, I'm no rich Texas rancher,
And I don't live in a palace.
I'd have tracked him down and whipped him,
'Cept my middle name is Dallas.

Terry Henderson

Terry Henderson

Terry Henderson was second in a family of eight children reared in Glenrock, Wyoming, after their father became the power plant manager in 1966. At 13, she began babysitting for a ranch family south of Glenrock, where she met her future husband Larry, the family's second son. She worked weekends and summers at the ranch throughout high school.

Valedictorian of her high school class, she served as student council president and earned a Wyoming Honor Scholarship to Casper College. "Larry was also attending Casper College, so I shared a ride to town with him," she said. They married that spring, following his graduation, and moved into a two-room bunkhouse heated with an old pot-bellied stove on his parent's ranch.

That summer, Terry worked as a wrangler at cow camp "which was around 7,000 ft. in the second mountain range. Camp was an old two-story frame house complete with a gas refrigerator, wood cook stove, old fashioned well with a bucket, and a two-seater outhouse for amenities."

While her husband tended the hay fields ten miles from the home ranch, Terry rode horseback through cattle, "doctored ill or injured critters, monitored the range land, kept bulls from gathering in one area, or fixed fences after bulls had a fight, as well as finding them when they tore up the fences." She also kept the salt well scattered.

Determined that Terry would finish college, the young couple spent their evenings cutting burdock for bounty so that she would have new clothes to wear to classes. The following spring, she enrolled in accounting courses. To save money, she rode a yellow school bus from the ranch to the nearest Casper junior high school, from which she walked to the college.

The couple spent that winter in cow camp, the year their daughter Starla was born. "We had an outhouse for a bathroom and an old hand crank pump from a cistern below the house for indoor plumbing."

She bought into the ranch operation following her husband's death in 1981, and decided to earn a degree in the veterinary field three years later. She then moved her two small children to Denver to take a technician's course. "I learned to take x-rays, give anesthesia, do lab work, assist in surgery, and much more." Armed with an associate degree in animal science, she decided to work with large animals, although "most of the work and money is focused on small animals."

Terry remarried and her family moved back to Wyoming, where she "converted" her second husband, Frank, "from a horse breeder to a cowman."

The Hendersons are also firefighters. Her husband drives a 6 x 6 truck while Terry serves as "the hose man." Standing on the back of the truck, she sprays water on the fire. "I've only been burned once," she said, a second degree burn along her jaw and ear. Fighting fires in Converse County, she helped to extinguish the Laramie Peak blaze in Albany County in 2002.

Terry wrote her first poem during her late teens and said her poetry is "pretty much a diary of my ranch life," which she keeps in a spiral notebook beneath her bed. Asked to perform one of them for a prayer breakfast at the Wyoming Stock Growers annual meeting, she was encouraged to continue performing.

Three books of poetry followed as well as several anthologies and a weekly newspaper column, "Country Concepts" that she has written since 1990. She also pens a monthly column in the *Casper Star-Tribune* and freelances for the *Wyoming Livestock Roundup*, a weekly agricultural newspaper.

"The Littlest Cowboy" was written about her infant son and "Ode to the Calf Wrestler" actually happened, she said, during a group cattle inoculation with friends and neighbors.

The Littlest Cowboy

My first ride off the mountain
was a young and tender age,
down through the pines and aspens
to the valleys full of sage.

We started at the cow camp
I was soon astride my horse.
My mom checked all the cinches.
She's a pretty good resource.

As we started trailing yearlings,
we rode both hard and fast.
But Mom was working with me
so I thought it was a blast.

Ten miles of trail before us
was a several hour ride.
But the pillow placed beneath me
helped to save my tender hide.

About half way, I worked to keep
my weary head from nodding.
But all was well because Old Red
just kept right on a plodding.

At 18 months, to stay awake,
it really was a battle,
And when I lost, Mom didn't care
because I shared her saddle.

Ode to the Calf Wrestler

T'was branding day and the neighbors all came.
One guy from the neighbors earned eternal fame.
Just after the gather we each took a post,
so Jack was a wrestler, where he's needed most.

Jack tried very hard and he worked without fail.
His partner was headin' and he got the tail.
They wrestled 'em steady an hour or two
before Jack got himself in a terrible stew.

As he grabbed on a calf and he thudded to earth,
Jack felt a tear split the length of his girth.
From zipper to back his jeans came apart,
but he kept right on wrestlin', bless his old heart.

A demure neighbor lady came to help us that day.
Straight-laced and old-fashioned was her usual way.
Would she care to vacc'nate? the trail boss did ask
To Jack's calf she went and bent to her task.

Too late did she see Jack sat in a pose,
Forgetting the shot, she quickly arose.
A retreat to the fire she staggered in shock,
her jaw fallen slack, unable to talk.

She handed a lady her half-used syringe.
She pointed to Jack, her face in a cringe.
Number two went on over to finish the shot.
When she arrived back, her checks were red hot.

It seems that not only did Jack have a tear,
but he also forgot to put on underwear.
Both gals got a view that they never forgot,
At our branding that day, they each got a free shot!

Garland C. Kennington

Garland C. Kennington

The Afton, Wyoming, native was a rodeo bull rider during his youth, but the one that sent him to the hospital in Bozeman, Montana, ended his rodeo career. He grew up on a ranch with milk cows, sheep, horses and five brothers and sisters. "I never did like the sheep and wasn't crazy about the milk cows, but I did like milk check," he said. "I had ridden a lot of cows at home and thought I could ride anything. I was wrong."

He enjoyed working with cattle and horses and wanted to live the cowboy life, "not realizing what that entailed." A job at the Half Circle Ranch in Geneva, Idaho, taught him what he needed to know "and how to treat people." He and his wife Julia lived and worked on the ranch for ten years before moving back to Afton, where he then worked in a saw mill. After a back injury and surgery, he wound up, not surprisingly, in the dairy business but another back injury in 1986 forced him to give up the dairy as well as riding colts, so he became an insurance agent.

Garland wrote his first poem twelve years later, inspired by an incident that happened en route to a family reunion in Afton, Wyoming, with his wife and Aunt Velda. The car broke down between Farson and Kemmerer, which triggered his creative juices..

"We had been studying about the Martin and Willie handcart companies of Mormon pioneers and the story about Francis Webster. He was so tired that he could go no farther. So he prayed." Webster reportedly said he felt as though someone or something had pushed his handcart through the sand so that he could struggle on to the next sandy area. "I thought about him as we worked over the weekend," Garland said.

On Monday morning, as he sat in his office, he felt that he should write about not only his experience, but "Brother Webster's" as well. The result was a poem titled, "And the Angels Came." Since that time, the poet has performed in the Wyoming towns of Riverton, Cody, Lander and Thermopolis, as well as St. Anthony, Idaho. He has also appeared at retirement centers, for youth groups, church socials, Christmas parties, family and class reunions.

The Riverton insurance broker helped establish the Cowboy Poets of Wind River, Inc. "We wanted to have an association that would promote cowboy poetry for the whole family," he said. "We've had sanctioned gatherings in Lander, Thermopolis, and the annual gathering in Riverton." At the time of the interview, he was serving as president of the organization.

"The thing that inspires me to write is the pleasure of looking into someone's eyes and seeing a light come on that says, 'I've been there and done that, too.' I love to entertain and help people see that it's okay to laugh at me and also hopefully at themselves. It's been fun to see the change in my own work and to see others develop their own talent and share it."

Garland Kennington feels that others like cowboy poetry "because it brings back memories or lets them experience a few minutes of a cowboy's life. They don't personally have to ride a bronc, or be chased by a mad ol' cow, or feed in the cold of winter, or ride drag. But a good poet makes them feel like they are there and often makes it comical besides."

The Title

They're known as buckeroos in the Great Basin
And as vaqueros out California way
They're called pen riders in the big feedlots
And cowhands in Wyoming, they say.

But there is a title that each of them covets
It's a title that's not freely given.
It's a title that has to be earned over time
It's a title toward which each is driven.

And if in your life you are privileged
To ride with one of these men
It's best to watch and to listen
And learn all the things that you can.

He'll teach you the ways of the horse and the cow
He'll teach you to ride and to rope
He'll teach you the ways to care for the land
And how to read ear marks and brands.

He'll show you how to treat women
In a kind and courteous way
He'll teach you respect for this country
But, you won't learn it all in day.

He will have earned the respect of his neighbors
By the way he lives every day
He'll be known and admired by the way that he works
Not just by the things he may say.

He may never hear that he's earned it
And wouldn't acknowledge it even if he did
For the title of cowboy is special—
It's not handed to just any old kid!

Spring's Comin'

It always seems this time of year
I can feel spring a comin' on
The horses have started sheddin' hair
And there are snowflakes in the air.

The cows have started calvin' and
The mud's six inches deep!
I don't know why I do this work
But then—I could be herdin' sheep!

It always seems that if I want to leave
And make a run to town
Some heifer starts to calvin'
Just as the sun goes down.

Then I tell the wife and kids,
"You'll have to go alone
I'll have to stay and nurse this calf
So it won't chill clear to the bone."

So I hang around the calvin' shed
And pass the time away
Then I miss the whole darn thing
While nappin' in the hay!

Lynne Hendrickson

Lynne Hendrickson

Lynne Hendrickson wrote her first poem after visiting Atlantic City, Wyoming, "a partial ghost town," where she spent time in the old livery barn. "It wasn't long before my imagination took over," she said. "I could feel as well as smell the former presence of the horses and visualize how it had been 150 years earlier."

Later, while traveling, she said her mind began to drift back to the ghost town and "a poem began to come together. I was still thinking about it when I pulled into McDonald's. Having no paper with me, I jotted down the initial thoughts onto a napkin over a burger and "The Livery Barn" was born.

The poem was later polished and shared with family, who encouraged her to submit it for publication." Lynne sent it to *The Western Horseman* magazine, "and the editor liked it well enough to publish it in the May 2002 issue."

She first performed her poetry in Riverton that year,

and joined the Cowboy Poets of Wind River. "I was promptly appointed as one of the Board of Directors," she said, "and was invited to St. Stephens Mission School to participate in a cowboy poetry seminar in 2002.

Lynne then organized and performed at a gathering in Lander, and participated in the Thermopolis gathering that year. Since that time, she has entertained at a Lander RV Park and has volunteered to entertain at the local nursing home as well as a Wyoming Cattlewomen's banquet.

She's also performed at the Global Café, a local Lander performing arts studio. Lynne was invited to perform for the One Shot Antelope Hunt Ladies Western Brunch in September 2003 as well as the Riverton Cowboy Gathering that year and the Lander Poetry Gathering the following February

What motivates a poet to write? "Many times it's only a picture or maybe a word or phrase I hear, but sometimes it's a mood. Occasionally I'll wake up in the night with an idea and immediately rise and write it down before it's lost. I enjoy feelings from my fingertips to paper."

Rod Steagall is her favorite cowboy poet. "I really enjoy the eloquent yet simplistic way he writes about western life whether it be modern cowboys or historical." Lynne's poetry has earned her a number of awards, including the New Horizon Award for best upcoming writer in the Wyoming Writer's traditional poetry contest as well as second place and honorable mention in Wyoming Voices 2003.

She also writes songs which she performs at gatherings and other events, accompanying herself on guitar. "Ridin' to Do" is the poem she considers her best "because it's so vivid to me and says so much about how a cowboy feels about ranching, sharing his life and then losing his partner/wife. It was published in the August edition of *The Western Horseman*."

Lynne thinks both readers and listeners enjoy the cowboy

poetry genre "because it takes them into a western scene and situation many can only visualize from afar and haven't experienced first-hand. For the ones of us who've been there and done that—it feels like home and we can readily relate. They're people from all walks of life." Those who don't care for the genre are those who either don't understand the lingo or care for that style of living, she said.

The genre can be improved "by educating and involving younger people. The old ways are dying out and they need to be taught and preserved."

The Lander Valley poet is a Norman, Oklahoma, native and the mother of three sons and two daughters, who have given her five grandchildren. An Eastern Wyoming College and Utah Trade Tech graduate, she serves as an outreach specialist for a mental health service.

Lynne's poems, "Ridin' to Do" and "Savin' the Herd" are featured here.

Ridin' To Do

Times were tough when Pa was comin' up,
tryin' to make a livin' on a spread.
Grandpap had homesteaded with a team 'o half broncs.
Hard work was all that they knew.
Built corrals, a barn, and trailed in the cows.
There was always a lotta riding' to do.

The years passed by, the grandfolks're gone.
Pa took up t'runnin' the place.
Brought a sweet bride to the old Circle L.
Side by side the work they embraced.
Through good times and bad they both stuck it out
making hay, pullin' calves and they knew. . .
Together, they'd make it and no matter what
there was always more ridin' to do.

Through the hours long and the income short
there was peace at the end of the day.
Pa, my two brothers and me drivin' in
talkin' pastures, cow prices, and hay.
After supper Pa'd go for the horses—
he always saddled up just two.
"Hurry up Hon, the sunset's a beaut!
We got some ridin' to do!"

We kids always knew it was their time.
They'd done this year after year.
The ranch was their life, they knew every hill.
Each rock and tree they revered.
Then Ma took pneumonia last winter;
passed away and we bid her adieu.
Pa kissed her good-bye, "Soon be joinin' ya,
got a little more ridin' to do!"

We went on together Pa, me and the boys,
workin' and doin' our best.
Pa just existin' from habit–
lost with his Hon laid to rest.
One mornin' he was late from grainin' the colts.
I found him sittin' in the sun,
Leanin' peaceful-like 'against Ma's headstone.
He'd got all his ridin' done.

Savin' the Herd

Tracks showed the rustlers headed
t'ard a canyon up ahead.
If Billie didn't get 'em
his herd could wind up dead.

He pressed his mount even harder,
the little horse had lots o' heart.
Bill hoped Buck didn't break wind,
the rustlers had a good start.

They topped the low ridge when a bullet
whizzed by Bill's hat!
He swerved Buck to a washout
and under the bank they sat,

Ponderin' what to do next
so's neither one of 'em got shot.
Bill follered the washout down a ways,
then up a low rocky spot.

He left Buck tied and went on foot,
keepin' his head down low.
He peered through the cedar trees;
saw two outlaws down below.

Sneakin' back he swung on Buck,
tore over the hill shootin' fast.
Hopin' his pistol didn't run out
and his pony's wind would last

He saved the herd as Buck galloped wild,
but turning' he had a wreck!
Bill felt the ground come up hard;
a wonder he didn't break his neck.

He rolled over and winced
at his skinned up knees.
Heroes didn't have this happen
in Saturday matinees.

Lookin', his gallant Buck laid there–
Bill worried just what to do.
This was a BAD predicament–
his stick horse was broke clean in two!

Pete Davis

Pete Davis

Born in Sheridan, Wyoming, Pete Davis was reared by his paternal grandparents following the death of his mother."My grandpa was 70 years old," he said. "He was an old Texas Trail cowboy who started a ranch at Cambria, Wyoming, now a ghost town near Newcastle.

"When the railroad opened the coal mines at Sheridan, he moved there and started another ranch to provide beef for the miners." Pete and his father moved to Kellogg, Idaho, where he attended high school, following his grandparents death in 1947. "After about fifteen years in different occupations, including cowboying, I realized I was getting pretty broken up body-wise and decided to go to college."

Pete attended Sheridan College and graduated from the University of Wyoming with honors and a vocational education degree. He then taught for a while in Sheridan before transferring to Riverton, where he instructed students for the next twenty years.

His first marriage produced three children. He then married Cindy in 1978. His second wife performs with him on stage and selects the poems for each program as the couple travels to each gathering in their motorhome.

"I know the first poem I'll do at any given program," he said, "but from then on, she selects the poems to fit the audience. Cindy's ability to select poems is uncanny, in that she seems to read what a particular audience will enjoy." The Davises have performed at more than 700 programs with audiences numbering as high as 7,000. All of them, he said, have been well received.

Pete's first poem was published in a national square dancing magazine in 1985. "This was important," he said, "because Cindy and I met while square dancing." His next poem, "Buy American Made," was published in WREN, the rural electric magazine.

The Davises usually perform an hour-and-a-half to two-hour program an average fifty times a year throughout the Rocky Mountain region. They also helped organize the Cowboy Poets of Wind River in September 2002, which claims some fifty members.

Pete said his motivation to write "comes from life," his childhood memories, personal experience and "happenings of cowboy interests." He's determined to keep the cowboy culture and philosophy alive. "I write anytime I have a few minutes, in the doctor's waiting room is a good place or anywhere an idea hits me. I carry a little notebook in my hip pocket."

Although he doesn't have a schedule, he writes custom poetry for funerals and other events. His work is not confined to cowboy poetry, however. Pete writes articles for church services as well as letters to the editor that appear in the *Casper Star-Tribune*, which he terms "ole cowboy opinionated."

The Davis's granddaughter exhibits a talent for writing

and her grandfather hopes she will develop an interest in cowboy poetry because she enjoys his writing. "Cowboys have always been heroes and folks still identify with them. So, when someone writes in the cowboy vane, it touches that hero vein and one ear is cocked to listen."

"Those who read cowboy poetry are not as much in the aware as those who listen to it," he said. "Cowboy poetry has to be heard to be truly appreciated. The reader-reciter brings it into life by their actions and voice."

The poet's work has been published in national and international periodicals and five anthologies, more than 1,000 poems during his career. A distinguished lifetime member of the International Society of Poets and member of the organization's hall of fame, he's a three-time recipient of the Pride of Wyoming Award. He has also been listed in *Marquis' Who's Who in the West, Who's Who in America and the World* as well as Strathmore's *Who's Who in America, International World Literature, Who's Who of London, North American Professional Western Performers of 2000,* and distinguished member of the *American Registry of Western Performers 2002.*

Pete Davis summed up his feelings about the genre with: "Keep it cowboy, keep it family, keep it clean is the motto we live by. "There's no need to be profane or vulgar in cowboy poetry. My grandpa could cuss the bark off a tree but he never cussed in public or in front of any woman. That makes cowboy poetry acceptable and welcome everywhere."

His poetry, "Measured by Number" and "A Time an' Place" are examples of his cowboy code.

Measured by Number

We've all experienced the child's
questions, how much longer?
As parents git experienced the
answer always gits stronger.
But when adults, horseback, on a
cattle drive begin ta ask,
Ya know cowboyin' has lost it's fun
an' now becomes a task!

A trail boss of dudes takin' cattle
ta mountain summer pasture,
Knows when they keep a askin', it
don't make time go any faster!
So an hour in ta the drive when the
question is asked the first time,
The boss comes up with a good
answer, though it is a little sublime.

About thirty minutes, we'll witness
the boss's call,
An' after about six hours that
question's been asked by 'em all!
But, ya got ta look at cowboy
philosophy in that answer,
Life is looked at, not as a whole, but
as one step at a time kinda transfer.

Ta the dude, they only look fir the
beginning' an' the end,
Fir they answer to the been there, did
that is of modern trend.
But the cowboys of old, an' of now,
do it in stages of time,
Fir they know there's a lot of steps afore
reachin' the end of the line!

An' while the dudes count all of them,
about thirty minutes more,
The cowboy on the trail takes it all in
stride, 'cause he's seen it all before,
An' he knows there's good an' bad
found in all them trail's chores
An' there'll always be times in life when
ya wish ya had thirty minutes more!

A Time an' Place

Ole cowboys have found when a
herdin' dudes ya ache,
With them things they learn ya,
while they're temptin' fate,
Ya try ta foresee them prairie
dog holes an' such,
fore they git ta cussin' you an'
all their bad luck.

We'd gathered the herd fir that
high mountain drive,
Up ta where the summer grass was
Jist a comin' alive.
We'd a made better time if we was
minus the dudes,
Fir them problems they jist seem
ta kinda exude.

We put about four ta ridin' drag
fir stragglers ta hurry,
Them cows weren't no problem but
them dudes gave us worry,
When we begin ta notice some
of them cows turned back,
So, the old hands went after 'em
with a yellin' and shoutin' attack.

All the while the rest of the herd
slowed to a whoa,
We finally got 'em gathered an'
bunched back up ta go,
The trail boss pulled them dudes
aside jist ta explain,
Some of the rules that were used
in playin' this here game.

One lady said there weren't no need
ta yell an' shout,
Fir she knew what keepin' control
was really all about,
Fir years in a classroom, to discipline
she weren't no stranger,
But the boss said, lady, them cows
don't respond to the snap of yur fingers!

Honey DeFord

Honey DeFord

Born in Casper, Honey DeFord was the only child of Harry and Agnes Stevick, a ranching couple who combined a number of homestead purchases to produce "a fine ranch" located on Antelope Creek between Douglas and Gillette. The creek lent its name to the ranch.

Honey's grandmother was born in Wyoming territory, and gave birth to Honey's father in 1895 in Cheyenne. A rawhide rope was given to her grandparents by Tom Horn shortly before he was hanged in 1903, and handed down to Honey. She considers the rope a treasure.

Home schooled on the Antelope Creek Ranch, she attended high school in Douglas, and the University of Wyoming. A rodeo participant, she remains a member of the PRCA and NPRA. She also enjoys training horses and has judged and timed many rodeos and ropings, including the National High School Finals for the past thirty years.

Although she has never performed in cowboy poetry gatherings, Honey is often asked to recite her poetry "as a tribute to a good friend or relative." Wally McRae is her favorite cowboy poet and she enjoys the work of many others.

Her work has been published in *The Wrangler* and *Tri State Livestock News*. Her favorite among her own poetry is "The Cheyenne River Trade" because "it was a funny poem about my husband trading an old gray kid's horse to Jim Reed for a crippled Salers bull." Unfortunately, she was unable to locate the poem.

The poet lives with her husband Jerry and has a son Steve Wuthier and stepson Hank DeFord as well as four grandchildren. She would like to be remembered for her Harry Jackson bronze titled, "Two Champs," and as an honest, hardworking cowgirl and good hand."

"Bandito Gold" and "Vi," written for a deceased ranching friend, are featured here.

Bandito Gold

I have a little buckskin horse
His name's Bandito Gold
I got him for a trader horse
But didn't get him sold.

Then I started riding him'
And rode him pretty steady
He's a super travelin' horse
And sure is always ready.

He'll weigh about ten-fifty
And stands at fourteen two
Whatever a bigger horse does
It seems that he can do.

And when it comes to workin' herd
He'll put a border collie to shame
Ears laid back and scootched way down
Duckin' a cow's his middle name.

Now Banditos's not quite perfect
I want you all to know
He'd never make a halter horse
Or win a quarter horse show.

He came from down Sonora way
South of the Rio Grande
His home was in the rocks and brush
Running with a Mustang band.

He still has rollers in his nose
And sees spooks most ever day
But he's become my number one horse
And is probably here to stay.

Vi

A few days ago a special friend of mine
Set out on a last long ride
She crossed the green Canadian hills
And up the Great Divide.

From the blue sky country of Montana
To the historic Rochelle Hills
Vi grew up and learned hard work:
Life was hard, without many frills.

She cared for children, horses and cattle
She was sure 'nuff horsewoman and top cowhand
From her homes on Black Thunder
and the big Cheyenne
She acquired, early on, a deep love of the land.

Whether at home or rodeos, near or far
There was never a truer friend that Vi
One was always welcome in her house or camp
You sure never left there hungry or dry.

We'll all miss Vi an awfully lot
Her family and friends she hated to leave
Rhonda, Will, and all the rest
But she would never want us to grieve.

She's up there now, where pastures are green
Ridin' a free wheelin' smooth-travelin' horse
She's riding with Francis and Ray
And son, R.C., of course.

Stephen Langer

Stephen Langer

"I remember my father saying that as long as he could sell a colt for what a yearling steer would bring, he would raise horses," Stephen Langer said. The Superior, Nebraska, native was the fifth child of six born to a farming family who raised a herd "of very good commercial Herefords."

Stephen moved to Wyoming in 1964 to attend college and never really left the state. "I wanted to be a cowboy since I was a young boy," he said, "and I literally fell in love with Wyoming and a young gal I met here. I know that God has created a lot of beautiful places, but Wyoming will always be special to me. It just feels like where you're supposed to be."

The cowboy married a fourth generation Wyoming ranch girl and he and Janice Lee settled in the Upton area of eastern Wyoming, where they reared two sons and a daughter. Both sons are married and one recently made the couple grandparents. Stephen worked in the oilfields while his children were in high school, but his first love is ranching with a little hunting, fishing and camping on the side. He's also a devout Christian and board member of the Upton, Wyoming Lighthouse Assembly of God Church. He says his poetry is a gift from God through the vessel of Stephen Langer.

He wrote his first poem in junior high school and "hated it. I thought [poetry] was for sissies and that it was punishment." Then in 1989, he heard cowboy poet Bill Wood "recite a poem that glorified God and I really thought that was neat." Later that year, he was driving home from work and "rhymes began coming to me," he said. "When I got home and got a pencil and pad, a different poem began so I took it down as it came.

"For several months they really came hot and heavy. I never could predict when or what the subject might be. I might be driving down the road, sometimes I would just get into bed. I had to get up and leave the room one time when we were visiting with company. When God gives one, I try to take it down. The reason for my poetry seems to be to glorify God."

Stephen has performed at various cowboy poetry gatherings in eastern Wyoming and Alzada, Montana, as well churches around the cowboy state. He has also taped some of his poetry for the ministry.

His favorite among his work is a poem titled, "My Lady and My God," which "tells about a miracle God did to get my wife's attention," he said. The poem and "Grady," a cantankerous horse, are included in this collection.

My Lady and My God

Have you ever heard of God
walking up Lone Tree Creek?
Well, He sure enough did one day
And He paused to pull off a real trick
He saved the life of a calf in the hay.

A mama cow looked on feelin' kinda sad
As my wife tried to convince her calf to suck
After a day and a half things are lookin' bad
This baby calf's really runnin' outa' luck.

Some things God pulls off for you and me
And some things He leaves us without
I can't always see what the difference might be
But His wisdom—I ain't goin' to doubt.

As a lady kneeled on a common barn floor
God touched a baby calf and said "Rise."
"Help" was what she asked her Lord for
But when he got up it was to her surprise.

He headed for dinner-time and was a waggin' his tail
As my lady watched—her Lord held in awe
He left all memories of bein' frail
And became a story that could—a cold heart thaw

Have you ever felt you were under God's smile?
In a place filled with peace—
plumb safe from all harm,
My lady said that God just paused there a while
"I could feel Him—His presence was in that barn."

Grady

I've been around horses all my life
Most I enjoyed but some have caused some strife
I've had friends that were sorrel, roan and bay
Some were calm, some nervous and one run away

I've had horses that could take a cow
to the calving shed
And one that'd poke a cow right through a gate
if you'd give him his head
I've been layed on and kicked and slid through a bog
I've chased wild bulls through brush
and even roped a dog.

Bonnie was a rip—but Sally—she's a real sweetheart
Lightning was always a bronc and ole Butch—
he'll do his part
I guess if you're around 'em enough things balance out,
'Cause I've had short ones and tall ones
and some were stout

But the one called Grady—I'll never forget,
To say he had a good start seems a mighty safe bet.
But one day when things seemed to be going good—
he got mad
From then on things seemed to go from good to bad.

I guess ridin' a horse is like bein' a Christian
See he's only my Lord by my permission
Ole Grady'd get along most of the day
But come a tight spot and he'd want to do it his way

And I'm sure I try God's patience a lot
'Cause when things don't go my way I tend to get hot
But may I always come back and bow before Him.
'Cause when I try to run His show—I know that's sin
So God forgive me and help me learn Your way
'Cause I know—before you—I have sinned today.

Now at buckin' Ole Grady got pretty rank
'Till one day he stuck me in a horse tank
Well, I come out pretty quick—
weighin' fifty extra pounds
But ya know that water really is softer
than cold frozen ground,

But today Ole Grady ain't eatin' my hay
'Cause he and I had a partin' – a – ways
See as with Grady my opinion merely
verifies the claim
And I know there is none greater than
His Holy Name
See I must remember that God is still God
And no matter what Grady thought—
I ain't no bull frog.

Robyn Schuppan

Robyn Schuppan

Robyn Lynn Schuppan first performed cowboy poetry for the Raton, New Mexico Arts Council in 2002 for their spring fund raiser, "Cowboy Nights," and returned the following year to deliver the opening address for the "Cowgirls' of the West July Fashion Show." Since that time, she has performed at the Cheyenne Early Morning Rotary, delivered the Cowgirls of the West February entertainment, and closed the summer as a featured artist at the Cheyenne Cowboy Symposium. During the fall of 2003, Robyn was nominated for the Rising Star Award from Cowboy Artists of America.

The Torrington, Wyoming, native was twelve when she wrote her first poem for her grandmother. A later poem was created for her sister's birthday titled, "She Cooks in Her Ball Cap and Spurs." Some of her best work, she said, has been written in the middle of the night.

The poet recalls writing a piece titled, "Wind," which she wrote for her father. She had wanted to "write something for him for some time" but the right words had eluded her until one morning while driving to work. During the thirty-minute drive, the poem came to her and she hurried into the office to sit at her desk. "That night, proud of my accomplishment, I rushed home to read it to my best friend and lifetime partner, Robb Bunten. When I finished, I asked, 'Well, what'd ya think?" His reply was, 'Well, it's short.'" So much for spousal critiques.

The cowgirl absorbs inspiration from those around her, whom she considers friends. She also gathers much of her material from her animals, including her dogs, a two-legged cat, bucking bulls, cows and horses. Other than her husband and animals, she most treasures her grandfather's Hoover Ranch and Wyoming state championship steer roping buckles, his steer roping saddle and rope can; as well select pieces of her grandmother's jewelry.

Robyn works in the Wyoming Department of Revenue, Excise Tax Division, following positions with the Wyoming Water Development Commission and the Engineering Department for thirteen years. In 1998, she left city government to "fulfill a lifelong dream of being on the road timing rodeos."

Robyn's featured piece, "Kickin' End" details a wife's frustration with menial ranch jobs which her husband supervises.

Kickin' End

It somehow has managed to remain
A Mystery to me time and again
Why it is that my Husband and Friend
Always lets me wind up on the Kickin' End.

Building fence, for instance, it never fails,
And I'm not able to shuck it
I carry the tampin' bar and mark the fence line
With stakes in a bucket
While he stays at the truck in the shade with water
And looks through the transit
Signaling which direction to move my pointer,
And take a stake and plant it.

When drilling the hole to place a post
He convinces me that I'm the gal with the most
Ability that is, to pull the stake and direct the auger
While he comfortably takes his time and sits on the tractor.

And when we run into that dreaded hardpan
He sets in motion for me his special plan
"Just take that bar and hook it on the drill,
And hang out here at the end,
Down pressure is what we need
Just be sure that bar don't bend."

Then planting the posts and setting those railroad ties
I drop them in the holes and square 'em up
As he stands off with eagle eyes
And has me hold, and fill, and tamp,
And straighten till each one sets straight and true
Then pats himself on the back at the end of the day
When both of us are through.

Calvin' cows and doctorin' cattle,
it's always the same
I'm left to my own devises as usually his game
"Get in there" he says "and run her in the chute
Because when you do it you look real cute."

He never starts a task prepared with tools at hand
Figures it's better to see just what you need, and
Leaves me hangin', "Now hold her there,
twist her tail, don't let her strain
I'll be right back with the pullers and chains."

He'll holler and ask where "I" put them
When I used them last
While the cow gets on the fight,
kicks me and I gasp

"Now speak up there,
I can't hear what you just said"
And trust me, if I had a rock,
I'd put a knot on his head!

When things turn messy in the corral,
As often times they do
He'll convince me, with words so sweet,
"Here, this job looks like you."

I'll dry off the calves, and sew up the prolapsed,
get everyone mothered and bedded
And looking about, find he's nowhere to be found,
because off to the house he's headed

I've run a million miles retrieving tools
He's needed whenever he fixed the tractor
He'll snap his fingers and tamp his foot
And cuss that I've gotten no faster.

We change back and forth between the auger,
the scraper and the disk
And every time it seems he yells at me
"To push it this way" and strain and lift.

When we bought our bucking chutes
We unloaded the panels and slides
He drove the tractor,
and with the chains on the bucket.

I hooked and plied
Each piece of equipment as it was lifted in place,
So I could bolt them together
Didn't matter to him that we ran out of daylight
And worked in inclimate weather

Modern day ranchin',
Often it takes both to accomplish everyday tasks
My husband is very good to me,
Because before he demands he asks
Would I like to help him,
Just for a minute, to finish a chore he started
He's not lazy himself; he too works hard
and is really kind-hearted.

So I don't worry too much about getting old and rude,
I figure things this way
He'll put up with me no matter,
Because really, what can he say?
He knows I'd gladly trade places with him,
my good pal and old friend
And he might just have to enjoy for a change,
being on "The Kickin' End"!

John Shreve

John Shreve

John Shreve's parents emigrated to the northern Wyoming border in 1886 in a covered wagon and were neighbors of John B. Kendrick's OW Ranch. "Sheridan was considered the home town to all the ranchers on both sides of the border," he said. "My father and my uncle both worked for the OW in their early years. Later, my father was wagon boss for Willis and Doc Spear who, like John Kendrick, held mammoth holdings on both sides of the line."

His father formed the A2 Bar Cattle Company with Doc Spear and prospered for several years until the devastating winter of 1918 when the influenza epidemic struck. "So, I think my roots go deep in Wyoming."

He grew up on the Crow Reservation and was schooled in the tiny town of Wyola, now a ghost town. "I finished eighth grade and then I lit out to cowboy on the Upper Little Big Horn for Ray Powers' 55 Ranch." John was sent to the Big Horn Mountains' summit to herd a few hundred head of black heifers, but at 19, didn't like the loneliness that went with the job. It was then he began writing poetry.

The following summer, he met a Sheridan girl whom he married that fall, eventually acquiring a "sizeable ranch on the Crow." They lost their ranch in 1985 and moved to Sheridan, where he then ran the Sinclair Service Station until 1995, when he retired. His wife Dorothy continued with the business until her death in 2002. He remarried the following year and now has fourteen grandchildren.

John is the author of three books, "not strictly poetry but many of my better poems are in my books," he said. His first poem, "A Cowboy's Devilish Dream," was written in 1952 while camped in the Cub Creek Camp. His favorite, however, was written about an event that took place in 1949 at the Crazy Creek Cow Camp and is titled, "The Poker Game."

Three generations of John Shreves have written cowboy poetry. "True cowboy poets write only of what they know, not some Hollywood version of shoot 'em quick, Jack," he said.

The cowboy has performed at gatherings in Cody, Sheridan, Cheyenne, Meeteetse and Buffalo, Wyoming, as well as Lewistown and Alzada, Montana, and Monroe, Washington. Six months after his wife's death, John was reading one of her favorite poems and was "suddenly overcome with emotion." He said, "I tried through tears to carry on but couldn't." Chuck Larsen, "true to the cowboy way, jumped up and finished it for me."

The thrill of remembering the life he loved so much on the range motivates him to write as well as leaving "a remembrance of my passing through this world." His favorite poet was Badger Clark because "he lived what he wrote about and he was there in the midst of the bawling herds and dust and was there when they set the plow to the land."

His most prized possession is his guitar and he sets some of his poetry to music. "I believe that people love cowboy poetry as it brings them to mind of days past that they never knew, but would give all they have to have been there. I don't know why but I can read three lines of poetry and spot the 'want-to-be cowboy poets' in the crowd."

John Shreve wants to be remembered for "all the compassion and help I can give along the way, and as a missionary of Jesus Christ, pouring out all the love I can."

The poet relives his cowboying days in his poems, "Whatever Happened" and "The Poker Game."

Whatever Happened

I have ridden trails,
That some of you will never know.
I have seen things done,
A hundred different ways or so.
Just kind of lookin' back,
It makes one a little sad.
When you think of years gone by,
And all the good times you had.

Where have all the good years gone?
They grow dim and very faint.
Only their memories linger,
Much like the fiddlers waft.
Old times go by nigh forgotten, Oh!
Where has the time gone?
Whatever happened to those good old boys?
Full of zest and song.

I wonder of all those trails I rode,
And landmarks as a youngster I knowed.
Those clear cool springs
Where the wagon camped.
Where the rope corral stood,
And horses stamped.

I can smell the faint odor of dust,
As the horses are roped out.
The smell of breakfast and coffee,
And the long waited, come and get it shout.

There was no place for dudes,
With their pant legs tucked in.
Who are filled with starry-eyed dreams,
That this is where the West begins.
No place for grippin' jelly bellies,
With all their wailings and moans.
Only room for the hale and hearty,
Who made this life their home.

The only things that's stayed the same,
As near as I can surmise,
Is the hoot of an owl on starlight nights,
And the screech of the eagle at sunrise.
But even these seem to be,
Gettin' all mighty few.
As though slowly disappearin',
As old cowboys do.

The Poker Game

I was workin' in cow camp,
On the head of Crazy Creek.
A ridin' with some other boys,
Archie, John, and Kip.

It was during the Christmas season,
Nineteen forty-nine.
We was doin' what cowboys usually do,
When stuck on the line.

After a hard day's ridin',
And a bite of darn good grub,
The old wood stove a' glowin',
It would really warm your blood.
The evenings would get pretty long,
And the story's would be told,
Some about girls and poker,
And others about findin' gold.

One night I'm gonna tell about,
At times I smile yet,
When they was gonna teach this kid,
To play poker, no limit on the bet.
I still had my wages, a hundred dollars or so,
The older fellers done figured out,
How to add it to their well.

My dad always told me,
Never tell all you know.
Always hold something in reserve,
And let your knowledge grow.
So when the boys said, "Let's play poker,"
I said, 'Golly, I don't know how.'
I seen 'em look kinda put out,
Then I ask them if they'd teach me now.

They didn't know my sister had taught me,
At about the age of nine.
I used to take her boyfriends,
For a nickel or a dime.
They tried to act so innocent,
As they told me a rule or two.
The game was seven card draw,
They figured me for a fool.

Josephine "Jo" Fulton

Josephine "Jo" Fulton

Jo Fulton's parents were early homesteaders near Recluse, Wyoming. The fourth of six children, Jo attended a rural school a mile from home before her family moved to Gillette, where she graduated from Campbell County High School. She then taught in a rural school that fall. During the summer she took college classes as well as night school and correspondence courses to complete her education. "But the requirements were increasing faster than I could keep up," she said, "so after five and a half years of teaching school, I did office work until my marriage in 1957."

Her next career was that of ranch wife and mother. In 1966, she "began an additional career when I started working as a clerk in the Upton post office where I continued working until my retirement in 1989."

Jo wrote her first poem in 1940 at the age of ten and still has the original pencil copy. Her second was written the following month for Mother's Day. "The Bronc Ride" was her first cowboy poem written forty-seven years later and performed at a poetry gathering in Newcastle, Wyoming. The poem won the championship rosette at the Wyoming Extension Homemaker's cultural arts contest for creative writing that year and was included in her first chap book titled, *Fulton's Folly*.

Jo has since performed at gatherings in Riverton and Sheridan, Wyoming; Montana and North Dakota, as well as a number of occasions in Newcastle, where she not only performed but was in charge of the gatherings. She has also been asked to entertain at the Stock Growers Convention in Cheyenne, Beta Sigma Phi state meetings in Sundance, the Rockpile Museum in Gillette, Extension in Douglas, Wyoming Homemakers, the state funeral directors conventions in Newcastle, and for many smaller groups on special occasions.

The poet describes her work as fitting into the following categories: "Truths, half-truths, might-have-beens and outright lies. Many of my poems are about actual events, and some are just my imagination. Quite a number of my poems are special orders and others were written when the inspiration hit me, or to take part in a writing contest."

Her second book, Homemade Poetry From A to Z, contains only one chapter of cowboy poetry while the other twelve feature a variety of subjects and styles. Her work has also been published in eastern Wyoming newspapers and the *REA* Magazine.

Writing talent seems to run in the family. Three sisters compose poems, although not cowboy poetry, and an older brother has written stories about his mountain climbing adventures. Jo's daughter, son and grandson have also written poetry, some of it cowboy.

The Upton Town Council presented Jo with a plaque in 1985, designating her the Upton Poet Laureate. A number of championship rosettes are also in her collection of awards and her Fulton's Folly won the Wyoming Historical

Society poetry award in 1991.

Jo has also won a number of "Spur of the Moment" contests and recalls the occasion when no other poet would enter against her. "Wayne Wipt, who was there to entertain as a musician, decided to enter so there were just two of us competing," she said. "He won with his first attempt at writing poetry and put my ego back where it belongs!"

The poet feels that more youngsters should get involved in the genre, "so there will still be people writing good stuff after all the old timers are gone. There are still ranches and rodeos enough to give them plenty of material to write about, and we should never discourage their imagination."

Jo's imagination is apparent in her poem, "The Bronc Ride."

The Bronc Ride

The cowboy just stood there
Just bursting with pride,
"Now look, and I'll make
A good eight-second ride."

His jeans were a mess,
All faded and torn,
His boots were all scuffed,
And his jacket well-worn.

He pulled his felt hat
Down tight on his brow
As he mounted the bronc
Calling, "Let us out now!"

They started to run
And circle and buck,
But the cowboy stuck tight,
It was mostly pure luck.

They twisted and turned,
Then twisted some more,
With a wild ride like this,
He should make quite a score.

They kicked and they jumped,
And they circled around,
I was sure he'd buck off
At the very next bound.

His hat bit the dust
As they turned on a dime,
But he stuck to that bronc
Until I called the time.

They bucked and they reared
All over the place,
And then he rode up
With a grin on his face.

They fell at my feet
Too tuckered to kick,
'Cause the cowboy was four,
And the bronc was a stick.

Andy Nelson

Andy Nelson

A Pinedale, Wyoming, chiropractor and occasional farrier, Andy Nelson composed his first poem in fifth grade, but didn't write his first cowboy poem until 1999. "It was a true story that my brother and I witnessed while shoeing horses and it was too funny to simply write an account. It had to be put to verse." He added that he finds "inspiration to write from everyday rides, wrecks and good jokes. I don't have a writing schedule, although I should, but will either write a little or daydream about ideas almost every day."

He writes only cowboy poetry. "Heck, I can't even get myself to write a letter. Cowboy poetry allows me to write without having to worry about spelling or grammar, and truth be known, I hate to write!"

The youngest of six children, Andy was born in Burley, Idaho, the son of a nurse and farrier. "My father was the Will James of southern Idaho. His stories and poetry were in a class of their own and you could never tell if it was the truth or not. He never published anything, but I have a file cabinet full of his own unique penmanship that I'm trying to decode and put into a book.

"My dad was a farrier all his life and I watched it literally wear him out by age 60 and that scared me a little. Therefore, I stayed in college and pursued the chiropractic field." He worked as a farrier, however, to put himself through school.

The chiropractor has performed in gatherings "all over the West and in Canada. I performed in the Kamloops Cowboy Festival last year and believe it or not, they asked me to come back in March of this year," he said. "I have run across a lot of people in different professions out there reading cowboy poetry. From agriculture folks to attorneys, and stock brokers to computer programmers, although not all of them understand it."

One of his first cowboy poems, "Making the Ride," concerns a young woman who, he said, accidentally hooked her undergarment over the saddle horn while trying to mount a bucking horse. "A couple of years later, I was performing in a large city far from where the incident occurred, and recited the poem. Come to find out, she was in the audience that night. Even though I didn't use any names [in the poem], I could hardly look her in the eye."

"Lack of Communication," is his favorite poem "because even though I wrote it and heard it hundreds of times, it still makes me laugh. The poem and a newly minted one, "Cowboy Poet," are featured here.

Lack of Communication

Times are tough, and it gets awful rough,
Trying to make a living off the land;
And as hard as we try, we barely get by,
It don't pay much being a ranch hand.

But we love this life, with all its strife,
So we do without most of the time;
We tighten our cinch, and pennies we pinch,
We can't even afford to turn on a dime!

So Mama and me, we both agreed,
To do our best with what we have;
We'd somehow make do, with a tractor or two,
And take turns when it comes time to calve.

But hayin' was hard, I'd come to the yard,
Many times, throughout the work day,
Just to repair or a break or a tear,
That I should have fixed out in the hay.

So we devised a plan, to save time as we can,
And developed a special signaling code;
I'd signal from a far, and she'd hop in the car,
Bringing parts and tools down the dirt road.

It worked real good, as I knew it would,
Until one day my swather broke down;
I signaled to her, that damage occurred,
And I'd be needing' some parts from town.

She understood well, what I tried to tell,
I made it clean with no ifs, ands or buts;
I need sections and rivets, a belt without divots,
And a handful of shear bolts and nuts.

At last I requires, a new set of pliers,
So I used the appropriate signal and stance;
But the answer detected, was not expected,
She grabbed her chest and the seat of her pants.

My signal was good, she must've understood,
So I sent aloft the message once again;
She replied once more, and I was quite sore,
When her response was exactly the same!

What's that mean, that one I've never seen,
Let's give this correspondence another shot;
It's real easy dear, bring the pliers here,
But a chest grab and butt slap is all I got.

I was smokin' mad, and wasn't very glad,
As I started through the field to the yard;
I'll get em' myself, they're just on the shelf,
The message wasn't all that hard.

I arrived in a huff, and I said loud enough,
I mean, "bring the pliers, for the love of Pete,"
"I know," she said, "ya darned bone head,
I was telling ya, there's a pair under the seat."

Cowboy Poet

A Cowboy Poet is a different sod
Some might even think him odd,
He loves to battle, with words and cattle,
And converses frequently with God.
He'd rather write than read,
A difficult and rare sort of breed,
He rode the range, fabled and strange,
And his first love is always his steed.
He paints murals with words,
Of life with family and herds,
His poetic prose, don't bloom like a rose,
Nor takes flight with winged birds.
He writes of the cowboy way,
Fading, but always here to stay,
As tradition dwindles, his poetry kindles,
The flame in a new generation's day.
Sometimes dying but never dead,
Old cowboys still live in his head,
With paper and pen, keeps alive the men,
Their folklore and what has been said.

R. G. Sowers III

R. G. Sowers III

Gerry Sowers spent the majority of his life in the south. The son of an army colonel and antique dealer, he attended North Carolina State University where he received his B.S. in agriculture before enrolling in law school at Campbell University. He then practiced criminal law from 1986 until 1999, when he contracted Parkinson's Disease.

The country lawyer moved his family to Wyoming prior to the new millennium following a visit to the cowboy state. The Sowers bought a small ranch in the Lander area where they raise a few animals because Gerry had worked with horses from an early age, and took part in Civil War reenactments along the eastern seaboard. "The most difficult thing I ever did," he said, "was to train horses to ride while firing weapons from their backs and through cannon fire and smoke."

Serving as a lieutenant in the confederate army, he spent several weeks on a battlefield site, without the luxury of a bath while a documentary was being filmed. "When I arrived home, even the dog wouldn't have anything to do with me," he said.

He survived ten years of reenactments without serious injury, but nearly died from injuries suffered from a fall when his horse Saber threw him at home. He credits the fall to Wyoming's rich grass which, combined with the grain he always feeds his animals, "energized" the horse out of control.

Gerry wrote his first cowboy poem in 2001 after finishing his western novel, *The Owl Hoot Trail*, and had asked writer/poet Jean Mathisen Haugen to review it for him. "Jean and I became friends and she convinced me to try my hand at cowboy poetry. I wrote several poems and much to my surprise, people really liked them. So I was hooked."

His first poem was based on a true story. "I did take a little artistic license," he said, "but people enjoyed the story so I made it into a poem. It always gets a lot of laughs."

One of his poems, "Little Joe," has been posted on the cowboy.com website and he published his first chapbook, "Another Horse and Other Poems." When he's not writing or performing, the poet cooks a mean pot of rattlesnake chili.

Humor is an important ingredient in the poet's work. At the Riverton gathering during the fall of 2003, he decided that instead of traditional western wear, he would don a colorful Hawaiian shirt and Sponge Bob Square Pants T-shirt with his jeans to make the point that "cowboys are individuals" who "don't all wear the same uniform." He repeated his unorthodox performance in Thermopolis the following summer.

Gerry recalled another gathering in his home territory when his friend Jean introduced him by saying that the Wind River Poets were not responsible for anything that came out of his mouth, because not even he knew what he was going to say. Prepared to recite a serious poem, he stammered and stuttered a while and then "finally got on track. She totally disarmed me, much to everyone's amusement."

It's not surprising that Baxter Black is one of his favorite poets. "His ability to tell stories and write poetry is amazing. You can tell he's been there and done that. He comes from the heart and he really puts all he's got into his poems and stories."

R. G. Sowers III feels that "people like cowboy poetry for its simplicity in dealing with ranch life and western Americana. Everyone has a little cowboy in them and cowboy poetry brings that out."

His poems, "Possalope" and "Little Joe," are more humorous when he recites them, but that's true of most cowboy poetry.

The Possalope

I was riding through the sagebrush
when I heard a rustling sound.
And I saw a curious creature
as my horse jumped and spun around.
My horse, he snorted, as that critter ran by.
I couldn't tell what he was,
but he sure was a fast little cuss.

He had gray fur but he wasn't a wolf or coyote
Cause I saw horns and hooves
as that critter ran by me.
He had horns like an antelope
and a long and scaly tail.

I took out my pistol, but my aim was off a lot.
Still that critter keeled right over,
just as if he had been shot.
I got down off my horse
and beside him I did crouch.
And then I noticed its belly had a little pouch.

And at that very moment,
four little heads poked out
They looked like antelope
but they had pointed little snouts.
The critter jumped up,
I stumbled and started to fall.
And that's when I realized
I was looking at a prong-horned marsupial.

Yes, that's the way it happened,
That's the way it was my good folks,
That's how me and my horse Sabre
discovered the illusive possalope.

Little Joe

Little Joe the wrangler don't wrangle any more.
He's done quit the outfit and he's working in a store.
You ask him about Blue Rocket
and he'll look you in the eye
And say, "That's my favorite pattern,
it's a very fine dry fly.

Little Joe the wrangler won't be caught dead on a horse.
He's up in Jackson, teaching a dry fly fishing course.
And he don't call a float a "bobber" or a "cork,"
He calls it a strike indicator like those folks do in New York.

He wears a funny little cap, and a fly fishing vest.
And he hangs out with the greenie, granolas,
and all those types of pests.

He uses barbless hooks. He's strictly "catch and release."
And he thinks it is a sin to throw a trout a grease.
He fishes with tree huggers.
They eat trail mix and drink chardonnay.
And when they see me with my worms, one will always say,
"Hey, cowboy, we fish with dry flies,
and that makes the fishing tougher."
"That's okay, my greenie friend,
that's more trout for my supper."

And little Joe the wrangler don't wrangle any more,
but you can find little Joe the angler up in Jackson,
working at a fishing store.

Gwen Petersen

Gwen Petersen

Gwen Petersen is the author of *Ranch Woman's Manual, The Greenhorn's Guide to the Woolly West, The Whole Shebang* (an audio novel), *Menus for the Cooking Impaired*, which she co-authored with Jeane Rhodes; *How to be Elderly, A Users Guide*, volume one; and a cassette titled *You Want Me to Do What?* co-authored with Betty Lynne McCarthy.

She also published five books of poetry, a poetry and song parodies CD titled *Shameless Satire*; contributed to numerous poetry anthologies as well as the following books: *Leaning in the Wind, Woven on the Wind*, and *Writing Montana: Literature Under the Big Sky*.

Among her other writing projects are numerous skits and plays including "*Justice Prevails or: There's a Fly in the Ointment of Love,*" produced by Spring Creek Players of Lewiston, Montana; a weekly column, "In a Sow's Ear" which has appeared for more than twenty years in newspapers in several western states, and a column in the online *American Western Magazine*.

Gwen established the first summer Montana Cowboy Poetry Gathering in Big Timber, Montana, in 1986 and serves as director of the Montana Cowboy Poetry Wintercamp held there annually in January. She's also the writer and director of the annual "Toot, Snoot, 'n Hoot" comedy show, director of the annual Sagebrush Writers Workshop in Big Timber, and a member of WWA.

Jean Henry Mead

Jean Henry Mead

Jean Henry Mead served in the Poetry in the Schools Program in Casper, Wyoming, with Peggy Simson Curry, and was intrigued with cowboy poetry after watching Baxter Black perform at a Western Writers of America convention during the mid-1980s.

She began writing professionally in 1968 as a news reporter/photographer in California and staff writer and correspondent for the *Casper Star-Tribune* in 1971. She also served as editor of *In Wyoming Magazine* and freelanced for the *Denver Post's Empire Magazine* as well as other magazines domestically and abroad.

Her nonfiction books include *Wyoming in Profile, Maverick Writers, Casper Country,* and *Westerners.* Her novels are *Escape A Wyoming Historical Novel, A Village Shattered, Diary of Murder, Murder on the Interstate* and two children's books: *Mystery of Spider Mountain* and *Ghost of Crimson Dawn.* She also ghostwrote two books and edited *What Our Parents Should Know: Advice From Teens, Wyoming's Historical Trivia* and *Wyoming's Cowboy Poets and Their Poetry.*

While serving as National publicity director for Western Writers of America (WWA), she founded the Western Writers Hall of Fame and served as WWA's secretary-treasurer. She also served as president of Wyoming Writers, Inc., historian for Wyoming Press Women, and is a member of Women Writing the West.

Photo Credits

Robert Roripaugh by Margaret Johnson
Sue Wallis, courtesy of the poet
Chuck Larsen by Master Imagery
Georgie Sicking, courtesy of the poet
Charlie Firnekas by Jean Henry Mead
Rhonda Segwick Stearns, courtesy of the poet
Mick Kaser by The View Finder
Jean Mathisen Haugen by the *Lander Journal*
Dr. Kent Stockton by Ty Stockton
Echo Roy-Klaproth, courtesy of the poet
John Nesbitt by Wayne Deahl
Ada McDonnell, courtesy of the poet
Ron Bailey by Jessica Bailey Cecrle
Gene Shea, Katie Star's Portrait Studio
Leslie Kelton by Janet Reed-Bradley
Verlin Pitt by Shirley Federer
Rick Pitt by Shirley Federer
Terry Hendrson by Frank Henderson
Garland Kennington, courtesy of poet
Lynn Hendrickson by Shirley Federer
Pete Davis by Cindy Davis
Honey DeFord, courtesy of the poet
Steve Langer by Eileen Nistler
Robyn Schuppan by Carol Martinez
John Shreve, courtesy of the poet
Jo Fulton by Olan Mills
Andy Nelson by Kevin Matini-Fuller
R. G. Sowers III by Jean Mathisen Haugen
Gwen Petersen, courtesy of the poet
Jean Henry Mead by Glam Photos

www.ingramcontent.com/pod-product-compliance
Lightning Source LLC
Chambersburg PA
CBHW070639050426
42451CB00008B/220